Turning the Corner on Grief Street:
Loss and Bereavement as a Journey of Awakening

DISCLAIMER:

This book is for anyone interested in the journey of the soul, with a specific focus on metaphysical interpretations of loss, trauma and bereavement. The grief process, while often painful beyond comprehension, can provide a critical path to a higher understanding of these experiences. The content in these pages assumes that the reader is interested in looking beyond the shock, suffering and sorrow of grief toward a non-dualistic spiritual understanding of human experience.

The unconventional views expressed in these pages may not be appropriate for those struggling with anger, guilt, fear or blame related to the death of a loved one.

This book is based on the author's spiritual experiences and perceptions, and is not a substitute for professional grief counseling.

The names in the personal stories included here have been changed. Any similarity to real names and real persons is purely coincidental.

Turning the Corner on Grief Street:
Loss and Bereavement as a Journey of Awakening

ISBN: 978-0-9623062-4-2

Cover design by Pamela J. Hunter

Contents

What the Experts are Saying About
Turning the Corner on Grief Street

"Terri Daniel offers new hope for the bereaved in her new book *Turning the Corner on Grief Street,* which will help guide grieving people from trauma to transformation."

Dr. Raymond Moody, best-selling author of "Life After Life," and one of the world's leading researchers on near-death experiences

"*Grief Street* takes bold steps in addressing the positive aspects of bereavement rather than just the pain and sadness. Teachers like Terri can help our culture rise to a higher level of understanding death and loss; an understanding that should permeate all levels of education, from kindergarten to medical school. Terri offers a new perspective on death and dying from the point of view of the bereaved *and* the deceased. Such a perspective leads us to a better understanding of the transition we call 'death,' and teaches us how to truly embrace life *and* death."

Dr. Joseph J. O'Connell III
Director, Department of Emergency Medicine,
Virtua Hospital System, Camden, NJ

"Few people have the mystical, spiritual, theological, professional and personal perspective as Terri Daniel to address the dynamic and life-changing experience of grief. Not only does *Turning the Corner on Grief Street* encourage us to evaluate our conventional ways of thinking about the nature of God, life, loss and death, it also provides practical guidance for walking the path of grief toward a more meaningful and satisfying spiritual life."

Rev. Gene Lovelace, MDiv,
Alive Hospice, Nashville, TN.

"Terri gives us hope that we can continue in relationship with our loved ones whose physical bodies have died. Human consciousness is evolving toward mind-to-mind communication while we are yet in the physical, and Terri Daniel is one of those leading the way."

Rev. Dick Dinges, Hospice Chaplain,
Virginia Beach, VA.

"Terri is a gifted writer and teacher, and brings profound sensitivity to her work in the community as a spiritual educator."

Lee Green, RN, MAT, Bereavement Specialist,
Covenant Hospice, Daphne, AL.

"Rev. Daniel provides an insightful, well-documented perspective on something few of us have actually fully understood - the strong, positive transformative potential of the pain of bereavement. We learn that grief is not only unavoidable, it is also fundamental for our own growth and development."

Piero Calvi-Parisetti, MD, medical doctor,
psychotherapist and grief counselor

"Terri is an excellent writer, and her heart shows through in practical and loving ways. I am so grateful she has written the books she has, and feel privileged to have been a speaker at her annual conference."

PMH Atwater, author and near-death researcher

"Terri dares her readers to do what they have avoided. She challenges those who are willing to discuss the "D word" over dinner to turn what we believe into what we *know*. Anyone wondering about what comes next should read this provocative book."

Sandy Goodman
Author of Love Never Dies:
A Mother's Journey from Loss to Love

To Danny,
the man behind the curtain

Acknowledgements

Many thanks and blessings to...

Austyn Wells, for wisdom beyond this world
Bruce Holsted, for generosity beyond this world
Carol Yurick, for steadfast awareness and dedication
Diane Goble, for coming back to tell about it
Dianne Purdie, for excellent proofreading
Eben Alexander MD, for introducing us to the mainstream
Jordan Justice, MD, for going to medical school
Joseph O'Connell, DO, soul friend and healer
Karol Avalon, who showed up right on time
Kay Conover, an unexpected and extraordinary teacher
Lori and Neil Shocket, MDs, for understanding the body
Marilyn and Martin Rose, beloved forever
Pamela J. Hunter, for consistently gorgeous book covers
Piero Parisetti MD, for wisdom that spans the continents
Raymond Moody MD, for wisdom that spans the eons
Rev. Jose Garcia, for giving me a chance
Robert Henry, for giving it form and shape
Ron Parks, for support in the face of adversity
Siggie, who may actually read my books someday
Spootie the dog, for love that defies description
Supporters of the Afterlife Conference, for making it happen
The Afterlife Awareness Facebook group
The Mystic Misfits of Marylhurst

Foreword

by Ron Parks
Grief Counselor and Facilitator for the
International Association of Near-Death Studies

I have been a member of *The International Association for Near Death Studies* (IANDS) for more than a decade, and for most of those years I facilitated a near-death study group in Salem, OR. My time with IANDS, my experience as a grief counselor and my study of near-death experiences has given me a unique viewpoint regarding grieving and the afterlife, as well as on reincarnation and related subjects.

Terri's brilliant metaphor about Grief Street addresses what is known in professional circles as "complicated grief." Hospice counselors and other experts tell us that when a griever remains "stuck" in one particular stage of grief for an extended period of time, the grieving process develops complications, similar to what happens in medical terms when a wound or illness becomes more serious. In those cases, it is important to mobilize additional resources to help the healing process resume. In terms of grief, this usually means approaching a specialized counselor who can help get the grieving process back on track.

Dr. Elizabeth Kubler-Ross taught us that there are five stages of grief... *denial, anger, bargaining, depression* and *acceptance.* She also taught that the grief journey is neither predictable nor linear, and that grieving persons progress at their own unique pace, depending on their temperament, the relationship to the deceased, belief systems and the circumstances of the death. The bereaved visit and re-visit the five stages in a fashion unique to each individual, and most experts concur that anger is the toughest hurdle.

Anger in the grief process can be directed in countless ways. It can be directed at the drunk driver who caused the crash that killed the loved one, or at a doctor who might have done better or arrived sooner. Anger can focus on the murderer or the cheating spouse who drove the loved one to suicide. Anger can also be aimed directly at the deceased person if his or her life was cut short due to carelessness or addiction.

Anger is also frequently focused on oneself for not taking actions that might have prevented the death, or for perceived inadequacies in caregiving or in nurturing the relationship. And of course one of the most common targets for anger is *God*, and with it, a litany of religious beliefs that no longer compute in the face of loss and tragedy. Anger can function as an armor that wards off the much more uncomfortable feelings of sadness, guilt and depression. It gives us the illusion of being in control of a situation where we feel we have lost all control. Anger creates the sense that we're *doing something* with our emotions rather than letting the emotions take charge. It helps us feel less victimized, and the more we hold on to it, the more we feel we are taking some sort of action to balance the scales. If we stay angry, we let the world know that we will not forgive or accept what has happened. We also use our anger as a way to honor the departed loved one; as long as we're angry, we are proving our love and devotion. Anger is probably the trickiest grief stage because it seems to have the biggest payoff.

But anger also has the unintended consequence of pushing away those who might offer help when we need it most. It can be a destructive emotion that triggers destructive behaviors, and is a close cousin to hatred and contempt. Hatred has been defined as "taking poison yourself with the intent of making the target person sick."

Unless we die very young, every one of us will travel the path of grief many times throughout our lives. We will lose a spouse, parents, friends, siblings, pets, and worst of all, we may lose our children to illness, accidents, drug overdoses, war, murder or suicide. Grief is probably the most difficult challenge we will face in our lives, but we are given very little instruction or preparation for it. In Western culture, people are uncomfortable talking about death, and often won't admit that they are in fact dying, or that their loved one isn't going to get better. Consequently we are usually ill-prepared for facing death.

Terri Daniel is no stranger to grief. She lost her son Danny in his teens after a long debilitating disease. She has worked for many years to assist the bereaved in the grief journey, and has written books and taught workshops on how to approach the grief process from a metaphysical perspective. Part of her teaching focuses on how to process anger by transforming it through a radical new take on forgiveness... the antidote for the poison of anger/hatred. She has had the good fortune to be assisted in her work by support from her son, whom she channels, and he continues to provide wise advice and valuable information from his vantage point on The Other Side.

This book is Terri's (and Danny's) latest effort to help people find a new way of understanding grief and loss, with a particular focus on the perils of getting "stuck" somewhere in their grief journey. Terri reframes the notion of grief as tragedy and presents it as a precious spiritual gift in disguise. But this is not an easy concept for many to digest, especially those who are deep in complicated grief.

This book was inspired by three weeks of dialog that began on Terri's *Afterlife Awareness* Facebook page in December 2011, when Terri posted a short blurb about an idea she called "Grief Street." The blurb spread to dozens of other Facebook pages, and prompted anger among several bereaved individuals. This caused a great deal of anguish for Terri as she tried to dodge the bullets, and I stood on the front lines with her as she battled the angry mob. But true to her teachings, the difficulty presented by this event resulted in an unexpected gift... the writing of this book.

Most "new age" spiritual teachers agree that we are here on Earth in order to attend Earth School, and we plan the curriculum prior to incarnating. We learn very little during the light, pleasant times of our lives. It is the times of major challenge, such as the death of a loved one, in which we profit the most and learn those precious lessons which are not learnable in the afterlife, where there *is* no death. The thrust of this special book is to explain those concepts in a way that comforts and inspires bereaved individuals who want to find the *meaning* in their loss.

Terri and Danny are always careful to point out the wonderful truth that our loved ones are never really "lost"... they are simply elsewhere, in another dimension, and that our relationships with them don't have to end, they only have to *change*. Terri also reminds us that moving forward in our journey toward spiritual awakening is the very best way to honor the memory of our loved ones.

Love NEVER dies. Nothing, even death, can trump love.

1. Introduction

"It occurred to me today that some bereaved individuals are so attached to their pain that they can't open up to other ways of perceiving their losses. They are immobilized at a fixed location on "Grief Street," even though there are fascinating new neighborhoods of consciousness, new languages and new vantage points all around them. They could peek around the corner and see what's on the next block, ride an elevator to the top of a skyscraper and see the view from the roof, or go down into a subway station to look at what's hidden below in the subconscious. But instead, they feel paralyzed and unable to move beyond anger, guilt, blame and victimhood.

"Grief gives us the opportunity to look into these previously untapped corners of our psyches. It's the hidden gift of grief... the extraordinary opportunity for growth that only a traumatic event can trigger. These events don't happen for no reason. They are not random, and they are certainly not punishments from a judgmental God. They are gifts of growth, if we are awake enough to see them that way."

Terri Daniel, December, 2011

___

On a snowy winter morning in 2011, I "received" the words quoted above in a meditation. I was so moved by this message that I shared it with the *Afterlife Awareness* group that I moderate on Facebook. It was a remarkable metaphor that beautifully expressed the nature of the work I do in teaching a metaphysical approach to death, trauma, loss and forgiveness. I knew that not every one of the group members would understand it, but I never expected the flurry of angry responses that erupted when the message went viral and spread to some of the grief support groups on Facebook.

While the vast majority of the people in my group are comfortable with out-of-the-box metaphysical thinking about birth, death and beyond, the group also attracts its share of skeptics, and also a good number of people who are struggling with the recent loss of a loved one. The skeptics are easy... they usually throw in a few comments challenging scientific evidence about near-death experiences and call it a day. But the newly bereaved – and especially the angry bereaved – are a different group entirely. For them, the pain of their losses seems insurmountable, and they are hemorrhaging from their wounds. Many have experienced terrible tragedies, such as the murder or suicide of a child, and most have not had the benefit of professional grief counseling or appropriate spiritual care.

Many also struggle with a crisis of faith. If they were raised with traditional Western religious doctrines, they might believe that God is supposed to protect good people from harm, and now that the worst imaginable harm has befallen them, they cannot make sense of how such a thing could happen in a universe ruled by a compassionate creator. Judeo-Christian theology asks us to see cause-and-effect as something over which we have no control, because in that way of thinking, cause is created by an external force that exists somewhere "out there," and we are the hapless victims of a remotely-located God that randomly dispenses sorrow, joy, reward and punishment. In this view, effect is our response to the events forced upon us by this humanoid (and frequently sadistic) god, so naturally this scenario leaves us little opportunity to make sense of our losses.

In addition to questioning closely-held religious beliefs and socio-political values, many of the bereaved are also forced to re-evaluate their beliefs about fairness and justice. If a loved one was murdered or died in a car wreck at the hands of a drunk driver, the event is seen as one in which there is a victim and a perpetrator, so it is natural to assign blame, and some bereaved individuals spend decades in the court system trying to bring the perpetrator to justice. But even in the absence of an identified perpetrator, the need to focus fault on something or someone can keep people locked into a lifetime of rage and indignation aimed at a person, at God, at the medical establishment, at society, at perceived perpetrators, and at themselves.

In my attempt to introduce the Facebook group members to another possible way of looking at grief, I unleashed a torrent of protest from what amounted to something akin to an angry mob. Many felt that I was demeaning their grief journeys, several stated that they will never find peace until their dead loved ones are "returned to them," and some called me a charlatan. One woman accused me of trying to profit from other people's suffering and exploiting my own son's death (he died at age 16 in 2006), and another said that I have no right to work in hospice since I have no compassion for the bereaved. One woman actually went so far as to post libelous comments about my non-profit foundation and tried to characterize me as a corrupt agent of corporate America.

Their anger was very real. But it was also very displaced. For three weeks my words fueled a Facebook firestorm in which I became a target for projections of pain and outrage from people who did not want to hear that the metaphysical realities of death are not the same as the emotional realities, or that grief has hidden gifts that can lead to sparkling new vistas.

Western culture conditions us to believe in victimhood, revenge and retribution in a world where wealth vs. poverty, sickness vs. health and life vs. death are arbitrarily apportioned. To suggest that these conditions may not be random and that suffering may actually have a higher purpose is not something that many grieving people are able to hear. It is more familiar and more acceptable in mainstream society to see a tragic loss as a random or meaningless event. Looking at it any other way is foreign to our cultural and religious references, and without the comfort and protection of those references, we are left out in the cold. Many of the bereaved are taught – correctly – that they will eventually heal; that help is available from support groups and grief counselors; and that they have a right to grieve in their own way for as long as they wish. But what they are not usually told is that they have a choice about how to perceive the traumatic loss experience.

Grief work is most effective when it strives to find meaning in the loss, and there is an enormous body of academic research that supports the idea that finding meaning creates a healthier adjustment.[1] When the loss can be viewed with an open heart – with tenderness rather than pain[2] – it can be seen as simply a change in the relationship with the lost person rather than the complete and total disappearance of the relationship. It is a redefinition of attachment rather than complete detachment. The relationship does not disappear. It just changes form

Although I have training and experience in grief counseling, I am not a licensed counselor. I'm an intuitive, a spiritual teacher and an ordained interfaith minister with a formal education in theology and experience as a hospital chaplain and a midwife to the dying. The education and training is certainly useful, but I am primarily a conduit for information that I receive, for lack of a better word, *telepathically*, which makes me merely a messenger. When I began the work of sharing channeled messages from my son Danny on The Other Side (you will find excerpts from some of those messages quoted throughout this book), I attracted a large audience of bereaved parents. I worked with organizations like The Compassionate Friends and Bereaved Parents USA, which was a logical match because we shared the common experience of losing a child. But over the years, as I acquired new knowledge, my message began to evolve, and I began asking my audiences to evolve with me, which is no small task for many of the bereaved. It requires a new understanding of forgiveness, a belief in the innate divinity of all things, the holiness of every encounter, a purpose to every experience and a view of ourselves as more than just our physical bodies and the personal dramas that play out in each incarnation.

For many people, this requires a complete theological overhaul.

There are hundreds of professional counselors out there who can gently and delicately guide the bereaved step-by-step through the grief journey. But I have come to a place where I want to focus on the *next* steps, and with those steps come many new questions. What happens when we don't want to suffer any more? What happens when we are ready to become different people and see the world in a new way? Who will guide the bereaved toward seeing their losses as part of a bigger system that works in harmony with the oneness of the universal mind?

If I just lost you with that last sentence, then this book may not be for you. But if the idea of looking at human relationships, attachments and experiences through a distinctive new lens appeals to you, then I invite you to join me here. Those of you who read my 2010 book, *Embracing Death*, may recall that talked about how I was banned from speaking at national conferences for bereaved parents because I wanted to discuss mediumship and after-death communication, which made the conference organizers uncomfortable. Now it seems I have moved into yet another realm of exploration that makes people uneasy, but I proudly accept that charter if that's what it takes to get my message to the masses.

I would never, ever ask anybody to dismiss or deny the very real pain of grief. But if you're truly interested in incorporating your pain into who you are becoming as a result of your loss, I ask that you consider creating a new vision of the universe with the added dimension given to you by the grief experience.

This book is all about that vision... the one we can see when we turn the corner on Grief Street.

NOTES

[1] Archer, John. The Nature of Grief: The Evolution and Psychology of Reactions to Loss. Routledge, 2002.
[2] Dembo, Leviton and Wright,1956 qtd. in Archer, 117

2. How Trauma Transforms Us

"Pain that is not transformed is *transmitted.*"
Richard Rohr

"Three highways into the heart are silence, love and grief."
Matthew Fox

"Until we can feel gratitude for our pain, we cannot truly begin to heal."
A channeled message from Danny

With the deepest respect for the very real pain of grief, the purpose of this book is to help us examine how the grief journey can break down barriers, open our hearts, change our thinking and create a more spacious form of spiritual awareness. I have learned through personal experience and through my work as a spiritual teacher, that grief and loss can be a magnificent growth experience that increases compassion, shifts one's focus into more positive endeavors, deepens relationships, enhances creativity and generates an increased feeling of connection to humanity and the spiritual world. As I wrote in my 2010 book, *Embracing Death: A New Look at Grief, Gratitude and God:* [3]

"Grief is like open-heart surgery. Nothing can rip us open, hurt us, scar us and heal us more than grief, and nothing brings us more valuable soul lessons. The primary gift of grief is that it changes us permanently and profoundly, and because we are never truly separated from those who have crossed over, their deaths invite us to enter new worlds along with them. Grief cuts to the core of everything that defines us, and exposes places in our relationships, belief systems, family structures and social values that have been crying out for illumination and healing. Grief shakes us loose from our spiritual lethargy and creates an opening in us that is highly receptive to growth if we recognize the tools and choose to do the work. If we nurture that opening, if we honor it and work with it, stretching and strengthening it a little bit each day, we can discover previously unimagined worlds of wisdom, and choose enlightenment over annihilation. Every one of us who's had a life-shattering grief experience has, on a deep metaphysical level, asked grief to transform us."

Trauma, grief and loss can completely dismantle one's beliefs about good and evil, security, the nature of God and one's place in the universe. To live in that dismantled state is painful and disorienting, and to remain in that state indefinitely could even be considered a form of psychosis. In many of my lectures and presentations, I talk about the ways in which human experience can be compared to the turning of a kaleidoscope. All the pieces appear to be separate, but with every turn, we can see that they are linked in a way that allows them to de-constitute and re-constitute in a pattern of perfection that unites them in oneness and continues to exist in an endless possibility of forms. The kaleidoscope imagery can be seen in many faith traditions, such as the Buddhist wheel of life, the Celtic sacred circle or the Native American sacred hoop, all of them expressing the cyclical nature of the soul's journey. It is an ongoing, eternal process of shifting, changing, expanding and contracting that forms a *perfect order,* which, when understood, can bring us to a state of unity with the divine. In this state, change can be embraced rather than feared.

But most people in the modern Western world have a preconceived idea of what that perfect order *should* look like. For many, it looks like a biological family unit with a comfortable house, a peaceful home life, a stable income and 2.5 thriving children. But when we scratch the surface of that picture, especially as professionals involved in grief or hospice work, we see that the kaleidoscope shifts whether we want it to or not, and frequently that scene unravels in one way or another. Mom might have an affair or lose her job, dad might get disfigured in a tragic accident, one of the kids might overdose on drugs or get killed in a war, and the expected (preferred) order gets turned on its ear. Some would see this as chaos, when in fact it's really nothing more than a *new order,* just like what happens to the pieces in the kaleidoscope. If everything in the universe is organic, moving and evolving, then everything *IS* order, in one form or another.

With every turn of the kaleidoscope, our rigid beliefs, established traditions and secure settings are shaken up irreparably. This shake-up is at the core of every traumatic event, and it results in a loss of faith and a loss of our sense of safety, order and continuity in life. When we no longer have that safe place to reside, we are exposed to the elements with no protective armor, no belief system, and no rules, morals or formulas to protect us.

It is a terrifying, dark, powerless place. But it is also a place from which a new way of seeing the world can emerge. If we walk naked and trusting into that place, we are met with superb opportunities to experience the world in a new way. Our beliefs and realities come into question, but if we're willing to re-evaluate those beliefs and realities, we can find a key to tremendous personal growth, both psychologically and spiritually.

The Dark Night of the Soul

There is a beautiful spiritual concept that originated in medieval Christian theology called "the dark night of the soul." It is based on a poem written by a by 16th-century Spanish monk known as Saint John of the Cross. He spent many years in deep meditation, and he describes the journey of the soul as it disconnects from identifying exclusively with its bodily identity and finds its way back to union with Divine Source (commonly referred to as *God*). A critical part of this journey is the loss of ego; the breaking down of all things comfortable, reliable and familiar, and the result of this breakdown is a joyful rebirth of the Self in a new light after the darkness has been experienced and transcended. John of the Cross describes it this way:

"The dark night is the inflowing of God into the soul, purging it from its ignorances and imperfections, habitual, natural and spiritual... God secretly teaches the soul and instructs it in the perfection of love. He prepares it for the union of love with God."[4]

13

Certainly the bereaved can experience a dark night of the soul, but grief alone – grief without transformation – isn't a true dark night. To suffer grief and trauma and to resist the push toward a shift in consciousness is to discard a precious and priceless gift. Of course suffering in itself does not automatically provide a more accepting, more balanced and more forgiving view of human experience. Sometimes it can pull us into regret, blame, guilt, anger and projections of "otherness" that stand in the way of healing, as you'll see in the following chapter. But suffering that results in a higher understanding of human experience and a new awareness of ourselves is a profound spiritual blessing. When we experience this, all our attachments break away. We cannot become clear conduits for divine love until we work on our own *stuff*, and grief, in all its wretched pain, forces us to do that.

If we allow it to.

Our loved ones on the Other Side want us to grieve fully and fearlessly, but they also want us to find joy again. Their deaths (and our grief) are designed to move us closer to enlightenment, and we must honor that movement by allowing ourselves to experience the ego death that is born from the dark night of the soul.

As spiritual psychotherapist and mystic Anthony DeMello says:

"If... they expose themselves in blind faith to the emptiness, the darkness, the idleness, the nothingness, they will gradually discover, at first in small flashes, later in a more permanent fashion, that there is a glow in the darkness. That the emptiness mysteriously fills their heart, that the idleness is full of God's activity, that in the nothingness their being is recreated and shaped anew...They will notice that they have a yearning hunger to return to this dark contemplation that seems to make no sense, and yet fills them with life."[5]

What the Dark Night of the Soul is NOT: [6]

- A mood disorder
- Depression
- A psychological disorder
- Frustration or alienation from one's religious heritage
- Grief
- Discontent
- Despair

What the Dark Night of the Soul IS:

- A sense of drifting, wandering, being lost
- A time when spiritual practices no longer satisfy
- A time of letting go, surrender, especially surrendering former spiritual truths or paradigms
- A loss of one's sense of reference
- A letting go of old identities, especially spiritual identities
- A lack of attachment to previous religious practices or traditions
- A sacred disintegration
- A sense of openness and humility
- A time of total dependence on the divine – even as one can no longer embrace previous images of the divine
- A time of unknowing
- A spiritual passageway
- A mysterious invitation for transformation

This list was assembled by one of my favorite professors at Marylhurst University, and the item that stands out for me is "Sacred Disintegration." At first glance one might think that we disintegrate when we face the most painful loss imaginable... the death of a child. But if we look more closely at the concept of disintegration, it is clear that it happens as a response to any kind of loss or change:

DIS·IN·TE·GRATE - *verb* - to break apart into many small parts or pieces.

Transitive verb
1. *to break or decompose into constituent elements, parts, or small particles*
2. *to destroy the unity or integrity of*

Intransitive verb
1. *to break or separate into constituent elements or parts*
2. *to lose unity or integrity by or as if by breaking into parts*
3. *to undergo a change in composition* [7]

Sounds a lot like a kaleidoscope, doesn't it? I'm particularly fond of definition #3: *To undergo a change in composition.* What a remarkable concept for grieving people! We can experience this either as individuals through our own personal struggles, or in small groups such as couples or families, or in large groups such as nations or tribes. We're all in the kaleidoscope together.

Here's an example of how we might experience a change in composition as a group or culture. Last week was the 50th anniversary of the assassination of John F. Kennedy (I was ten years old at the time). There was a flurry of media reporting on this momentous milestone, and I was compelled to write the following blog post, which beautifully expresses the idea of a change in composition:

"The Kennedy assassination is a perfect example of how a grief experience can move us toward increased awareness and transformation. That event marked the beginning of a veil of ignorance being lifted from America. The post-war fantasies of security and status quo began to crumble, and along with it, our reliance on materialism, white male supremacy, sexual repression, racism and religious dogma to shore up the illusion of safety. This left an entire generation questioning its political, social, spiritual and personal reality. It was the beginning of the radical 1960s, during which so many inviolable institutions and traditions were broken down and re-examined. In this sense,

Kennedy was a true martyr. I'm sure he had no conscious awareness of how his death would move us forward in our evolution, but metaphysically speaking, his soul certainly knew. His death was a gift of awakening to America."

Can you see the spiritual logic here? America experienced a dark night of the soul as a result of this event, and the world at large experiences this with every war, every natural disaster... *every turn of the kaleidoscope.* Our "composition" is altered again and again as life rolls on. The world is still just as full of struggle as it ever was, because shifting awareness is not about removing conflict and making things "all better." It is about making us more aware of how things work, and the precious awareness we gain is irreversibly transformative.

I recently came across the work of a woman named Evelyn Underhill (1875-1941), a spiritual pioneer who talked about the "Five Mystical Stages of Development."[8] These stages follow a mystic's journey from identifying solely with the physical world and the desires of the ego to an ultimate realization of oneness with the divine... a journey that is frequently triggered by trauma. As I studied this, I saw in these stages the potential for them to replace – or work alongside – the five stages of grief as defined by Elizabeth Kubler Ross in her 1969 book *On Death and Dying* (denial, anger, bargaining, depression and acceptance). I've taken the liberty of assigning my interpretations to Underhill's stages as they might apply to turning the corner on Grief Street.

1. Awakening or Conversion
This is where the transition to a spiritual rather than a material understanding of experience can begin. It is commonly activated by a dramatic or tragic event, which could be a specific grief event, such as the death of a loved one or perhaps a divorce, job loss or an extreme personal violation of some kind, such as rape or other violent encounter. We can no longer live in a bubble. We can no longer be oblivious. We are no longer separate from the "other." Our sense of safety is shattered, and we become aware of our vulnerability and the fact that we cannot be protected from harm, despite what our beliefs and ideals may tell us. As an example, we

believe our children are safe at school until a madman bursts in with an automatic weapon.

2. Purification (or Purging) of the Self

Extreme disillusionment. Ordinary reality is turned inside out, our familiar identities are stripped away, and we are completely exposed with nothing to cling to. There is nothing to rely on but our own inner wisdom, but at this stage, our wisdom is on trial. We don't know what to believe anymore. The ego is no longer in control, and eventually we will have the choice to either cling desperately to it or allow it to dissolve and render us formless and empty. But for now, we are a blank page. Using the example of the school shooting, we are numb and in shock. It is surreal. We are decomposing... in *purge-a-tory.*

3. Illumination

If we allow ourselves to accept and experience the "decomposition" of stage two, we may begin to allow our definitions of self, belief, habits, relationships, God and the universe to slowly shift. In this allowing, illumination can begin. We may be receiving messages, guidance and visions in dreams. This is also when many bereaved people start to explore alternative spiritual views by reading books about near-death experiences and questioning traditional notions of heaven vs. hell, or total annihilation vs. the presence of a soul that lives on after death.

4. Surrender (or the Dark Night of the Soul)

Even while the light of illumination beckons, a dark night of the soul is necessary. We have been stripped of all that is familiar, but now what? Former realities, relationships and structures no longer serve us. Friendships, marriages, physical health, financial resources and communities begin to shift and/or disappear, and despite our attempts at control, we can't stop it, because the momentum is too strong. The door has been opened to another way of looking at the journey.

5. Union

What does union with the divine look like? Because words cannot even begin to describe it, it is easier to describe what divine union is *not*. It is *not* a state of absolute non-conflict or ease. There will be still be conflict and pain, and life will go on. You'll still need to earn a living, manage relationships and clean the bathroom. But you'll do it *differently*. It is a state of grace in which we seek balance rather than control. We accept loss and tragedy as part of that balance rather than seeing it as random, meaningless or punitive. Everything is seen with a mystical, spiritual view rather than a material view. We forgive everything, always, without exception. Now, instead of being concerned about or afraid of the "other," we realize that there IS no other.

You will see many examples of where people are in this process as you read the comments in the following chapters. Some have moved into union, while others are traversing the path at various stages and various speeds. Some appear to be stuck at one stage or another, similar to what can happen with Kubler-Ross' stages of grieving, but in spiritual time, we can never be stuck, because the journey of the soul is endless, and time is not linear. The journey of the soul is a circle, not a line or ladder, and we all move at our own pace according to a curriculum that is perfectly suited to our own unique growth plan.

Can you consider taking a moment to imagine that the grief and loss in your own life might have a similarly grand purpose?

NOTES

[3] Daniel 2010, 61
[4] Book 2, chapter 5 - www.ccel.org/ccel/john_cross/dark_night.viii.v.html
[5] DeMello Anthony. *Sadhana: A Way to God*. New York. Doubleday Dell.1998. Print.
[6] Schroeder, Marylhurst University, SPP 426-Western Mysticism, Fall 2013.
[7] http://www.merriam-webster.com/dictionary/disintegrate
[8] http://indigo.ie/~peter/underhill.html

3. The Conversations

As a foundation for understanding how challenging it can be to find the hidden gifts in suffering, I have elected to share some excerpts from the Facebook string that inspired this book. The comments you'll read here are both disturbing and enlightening, because they show us how anger – and a fierce attachment to that anger – can build walls and keep us locked into a very uncomfortable reality.

This chapter will be of particular interest to bereavement professionals, because the conversations that follow are the raw, unedited responses to my original *Grief Street* post on Facebook, and they provide a clear, uncensored look into the pure heart of grief. Some of the comments are quite supportive, but those only served to trigger more angry responses. Interestingly, the angry responses actually validated my point about being stuck on Grief Street. They provided enormous insight into how some bereaved individuals might react when invited to see their grief in a different light.

It is important to bear in mind that this Facebook group was dedicated to after-death communication and spiritual exploration. It was designed for spiritual inquiry, and not intended to function as a grief recovery forum. But since many of the bereaved are truly interested in learning about the world beyond death (especially if it promises the possibility of communication with their departed loved ones), they often find their way into spiritual/metaphysical groups such as mine in the hope of finding some help in making contact. The angry comments you'll see here came from a small minority – six or seven people out of 1200 active members at the time – that would have been better served by one of the many grief-focused groups available on Facebook.

I have reproduced the following comments exactly as they were written, unedited and uncorrected for grammar, spelling and punctuation. The names have, of course, been changed.

From Cheryl:

Teri, I agree with what you wrote about grief street and although it took me years I came to realize that my son's transition was a gift because it forced me to stretch beyond my borders. I kept this bit of information to myself though and dared not to mention it for fear that I would be "judged" by others for thinking this way. But for the last few years I have come out of the closet and I can now say "yes, my son's transition was a gift to me on some level, and maybe there was a reason for it." I now think maybe my son's spirit chose this experience to facilitate our family' soul's growth. I have felt like this for some time now.

From Jane:

I too absolutely agree with you Terri – for whatever reason though we have been able to forge a new connection with our children on the other side ... and that makes the grief much easier to bear.

From Don:

Terri, are you saying that a mother whose child has just been killed in a car wreck, who is standing in her house with a bottle in one hand and a gun in the other wanting to kill herself because her pain is unbearable, should NOT be angry? I'm sorry Terri, but you are a false prophet. I would hate to be one of your hospice clients.

From Mary:

I have grabbed this information, dissected it and kept the things that spoke truth to my soul and thrown away the rest, but oh my, at almost three years I realized all I've learned and all the truths I finally see are only found on "Grief Street."

From Joan:

Profit from another's pain is your game Terri. Did you lose a child? I don't think so. Or if you did, your child was not a big priority for you. I'm a resident of grief street, so what?

From Karen:
I'm sorry, but I refuse to believe that my precious son was meant to die. Children are not supposed to die before their parents.

From Doris:
I don't care about growth. I just want my daughter back. I think all this spiritual talk is a bunch of crap and you only say this because you are denying your own pain. Wouldn't you give anything to have your son back with you? What could be more important than that?

>   My response to Doris:
>   Doris, the reality is that I *can't* have my son back (at least not in physical form). And there is nothing I can "give" to change that. Think about this... if our loved ones choose – at whatever level those choices are made – to leave the physical plane in order to follow their spiritual growth paths, and we would do anything to have them back where we want them (even giving up our own growth), then doesn't that make it all about US?
>
>   In my view, that kind of attachment stops us from moving forward. Nobody can interrupt another's spiritual advancement. Our grief cannot hold our loved ones back from their journeys, but we can hold *ourselves* back by refusing to accept what happened.

From Don:
What kind of mother are you Terri? You are saying that it's OK with you that your son died and that you accept it completely? I will NEVER accept that my child died. All I want is to have him back here with me. Why wouldn't you want that? What's wrong with you?

>   My response to Don:
>   Don, in answer to your question, would I prefer to have my son here on earth with me? Of course I would, but I don't live in that place because I know it's not possible. From where I stand today, because I see things so differently than I once did, I

completely accept that he is where he is. Bringing him back is obviously not an option, and besides, I believe his soul had an intention, and he followed it. So I am now able to support him in that. I would not impose my will upon him. I honor his intention to be wherever he chooses to be, on earth or in heaven. I see his soul as equal to all other souls, and I don't see him as a child without wisdom or experience. He has far more of both those than I do.

From Laura:

Don... settle down please. It seems obvious to me that you are venting your anger toward someone who is brave and honest enough to put her truth out there. We need people like Terri in this world. I for one thank the heavens to have been led to her. You have made it very clear that her modus operandi is not of your liking... maybe someday when your pain has plateaued or when you can find moments of respite, you will see her intentions differently - for what they truly are: to bring forth an awareness I for one found indispensable to my growth and survival after the death of my only child.

From Karen:

Terri, you are saying that I am failing at my grieving process? That my pain is holding my child back from his spiritual growth? The fact that I am still sad and angry after five years, according to you, is a failure. How dare you say this to me. I will grieve any way I want to for as long as I want to, and I don't need spiritual "teachers" like you to tell me I'm doing is wrong.

My response to Karen:

Karen, I'm not aware of any language being used here that implies success or failure. Nothing like that has been said. There *is* no failing or succeeding. No wrong or right. No timetable and no judgment. And I specifically said, "Nobody can interrupt another's spiritual advancement. Our grief cannot hold our loved ones back from their journeys." Please re-read what I wrote.

We're all journeying together, like pieces in a kaleidoscope. I happen to believe that we all come from a higher plane, and we go back there between incarnations to bring our acquired wisdom and experience back into the collective. It's a continuing cycle of expansion. But I wouldn't try to convince you or anybody else to believe this way. You are free to look at it any way you like. I would only suggest that we all stop and think about why we believe what we believe, and what the possible alternatives are.

If we don't come from a higher plane of consciousness to learn about ourselves via physical experience, then where DO we come from, what are we, and why are we here? Some people think we're here for no reason at all, just to live for a few years and then disappear into nothingness. Some people think we're here just to procreate and keep humanity alive. Some people think we're here to do good deeds so we can go to heaven. And other people see it as a huge organic, evolving panorama of energy levels, vibratory frequencies and realms of consciousness. I have only offered a glimpse into my personal view. No offense was intended.

From Ron:
It is important that we move through the stages of grief to reconstitute ourselves after a loss, though there is no timeline or required sequence for this. Some people, especially if the death was tragic or violent, spend decades in the anger stage, and while they are certainly free to do that for as long as they like, it can inhibit them in a number of ways, by affecting their health and other aspects of their lives. It can also close down the conduit for communication if they're hoping to receive messages from their loved ones on the Other Side. When people can't move past anger, it is usually because they have not had proper grief counseling to

help them deal with the loss. Sadly, in our culture, death is kept in a dark closet, and most people deal with it more or less alone without any guidance from professionals who know how to help.

From Anne:
I don't buy grief is a gift either, and would trade everything and anything to have my child back. The original post appears arrogant and condescending, and although that may not have been the intent, at the point it became clear that others found it offensive there was a choice to defend it or apologize.

From Mickey:
I will never be able to call the death of my child a gift. I've learned many things since she passed and will continue to learn more, but like Don I too feel life without our child is in not a gift. I struggle to understand and piece it together yes I get that, but it isn't tied up in a pretty little bow.

From Linda:
Terri, is your agenda to enlighten, or are you just building an empire for yourself?

From Ron:
If the negative comments are being directed at the content of Terri's posts, then they would also apply to the posts I'm offering in support of her. I just wish to tell you that we both make our comments from the depth of love and compassion in our hearts, because we are trying to help. We have both been trained in grief counseling and are extensively read in the area of grieving. Everyone grieves at their own pace, and visits and re-visits Kubler-Ross' five stages of grief at various times. It is not a linear process. It is definitely possible to get "stuck" in one of those stages, and when that happens, it is helpful to use a counselor to assist you to get the process moving forward again.

Anger is one of the stages, and it is also anger that acts as a sort of psychic "armor" that we use to protect us from the much more painful feelings of sadness and loss. So it can be easier to hang onto anger because it is more comfortable than sadness and loss. But if we are to complete our process of grieving, it is necessary to give up the false protection of anger and allow ourselves to feel the more difficult feelings of sadness and loss.

My response to Ron's comment:
I believe what Ron is saying is that at some point, we need to move beyond our paralysis and find a reason for these events... a meaning in the tragedy. Otherwise, we spend our lives walking around in shock and wondering why such a terrible thing could happen to us. But what if we could see the situation in a new way that actually begins to make sense? If we can detach from our belief in randomness, perhaps we can understand the circle of life – including unbearable loss and tragedy – from a different perspective.

From Emma:
My son made his journey in 2006. I had already had two husbands cross, but it didn't prepare me for my 23 yr old son's death. I KNEW, after years of studying quantum physics and reading about the multiverse, that there was no death. But I knew it in my head, not my heart. I had so many signs from my son it was impossible to disregard them. I know there is no death. I do not think in linear time anymore. I am aware that my son, my husband, everyone who has stopped using their vehicle (body), is consciousness that is very much alive. We just transition. So, yes, I am at a place where I know my son is very much alive, more so than ever. He is Home. But that is where I am now. I respect now that each of us has our own personal journey and honor each one as divine.

<u>My response to Emma</u>:
Thank you, Emma. Yours is a beautiful testimony of a grief journey in which meaning and increased understanding is realized. Many blessings on your continued explorations.

<u>From Karen:</u>
I had someone say to me after about 2 years, "The old Karen is finally back." I said, "the old Karen will never be back."

<u>From Ron:</u>
Karen, that sounds like a very positive comment. To that person, it must have seemed that you had made a lot of progress in your grieving journey. Perhaps you have made more progress than you realize. You are now the "new" Karen! And that's exactly what Terri is trying to say.

<u>From Karen:</u>
If we come to earth to learn, why do we have to learn from painful experiences and so much loss? How can so much negativity raise our vibrations? It just makes us angry and miserable.

<u>My response to Karen:</u>
I think you just answered your own question Karen. If we come here for leaning and raising our vibrations, why *wouldn't* we experience the whole range of possibilities, including loss, trauma, pain, etc? We cannot learn without conflict. Both positive and negative are necessary, like the positive and negative charges on a battery. These are the experiences that challenge us the most, and from those challenges, we stretch, expand and grow. We did not come to earth in search of a conflict-free existence. We came here in search of experience and expansion.

From Don:
So now you're saying that life is all about pain and conflict Terri? Don't you know anything about positive thinking? You are the most negative person I've ever encountered.

From Paula:
After 7 years, I am still grieving, but I have learned how to hide the pain.

My response to Paula:
Consider this Paula... instead of hiding the pain, it's about *integrating* the pain into the wholeness of who you are. As difficult as is, the helps to create our personalities, our evolving souls, the way we love and interact, the way we see the world and many other facets of our human experience. It makes you a new person, as Karen said.

From Don:
Why would you want to integrate pain into your personality? Pain is negative and should be avoided. You are one crappy spiritual teacher Terri.

From Karen:
I have a problem with this conversation. Every time I write a question on grief I tend to attract the same people that want to lecture to me and force their points of view on me. I knew this question would attract those people. I feel like I am being preached to by the converted that cannot see past their own ideas. I appreciate your ideas but you have no proof that they are real. I am a grieving mother trying to make sense of this world and why what has happened .I do not need to be judged on how i am dealing with my grief. It is hard enough as it is.

From Rachel:

I once asked a medium, angrily, What could we possibly learn from this horrific pain?....I was told that a parent who loses a child learns the lesson of pure and true love.....I didn't understand at the time but I have learned that I must now love my son with not just my heart, but with all of my soul.....it is the purest kind of love... No greater love....no greater loss.

From Karen:

I love my son with all my soul as I did before he left.

My response to Rachel and Karen:

Rachel's medium is correct. It's a completely different kind of love. It is a spiritual love, not an earthly love. And in that love we recognize that every soul follows its own path, whether or not that path makes US happy. And in learning to release the people we love to their paths, we can find peace.

There were about 300 total comments in this string, and the conversation continued for several weeks. The comments I selected to share here most clearly express the divisions among the people who were posting. I was amazed when I realized the extremes that were being expressed, especially by the people who, years or even decades after the loss, were still in the 'bargaining" stage, wishing they could "give anything" or "trade anything" to have their loved ones returned to them.

I cannot imagine a better illustration of life on Grief Street.

4. God Does Not Have an Opinion

In my 2010 book, *Embracing Death: A New Look at Grief, Gratitude and God*, I posed the following question:

> **Q:** How could God let this terrible thing happen?
> **A:** It depends what you think God *is*.

This mystery confounds us when we face extremely painful events, even if those events don't involve us directly. We ask this question from a distance when we hear about a Tsunami in Indonesia that killed more than 230,000 people in 14 countries, an earthquake in Haiti killing 85,000, or a school shooting in which a madman guns down first-graders. And if we happen to be present for these events personally, the question is even more likely to lead us to a traumatic loss of faith and a shattered sense of safety in the world.

Since Judeo-Christian theology rules religious thought in Western culture, we are generally boxed into a belief that sees God as either punishing and vindictive, or loving and all-forgiving. Because these two "personalities" are at opposite ends of the spectrum and directly conflict with one another, we are faced with a quandary. Is God loving and forgiving, or does God punish us if "he" is unhappy with our behavior? Or perhaps there is a third possibility... *does God arbitrarily dispense suffering for no reason?*

If the religious teachings we learned in Sunday school are taken at face value, then this contradiction is glaringly obvious. The angry god of the Hebrew Bible thinks nothing of wiping out innocent people on whim, while the kinder, gentler god of the New Testament "loves us so much that he sent his only son to die for our sins." But how do either of these ideas help us understand and cope with tragedy in our own lives? In fact, how do they help us understand anything at all?

They don't. In fact, they fail miserably, because none of that is the truth about God. Those are mythical concepts and magical characteristics assigned to a humanized depiction of a non-physical, utterly *neutral* energetic force. In other words, those ideas are not meant to be taken literally! God is not a person, not a *he* and not a judge. God cannot love or hate, rule, conquer, punish or reward. God does not have an opinion, because God is not a man in the sky who behaves like a human being. God is an "it," not a "he."

I once said that to a woman at one of my workshops, and she became deeply upset about my use of the genderless pronoun "it" instead of the traditional "he." She shouted at me like an eight year-old in a schoolyard brawl, "God's going to be angry that you called him an 'it!' You better take that back, or you'll be sorry!"

On my flight home from that workshop, I kept wondering what she thought God would do to me if I didn't take back my insult. Would my plane crash as punishment for calling God an "it?" Would the other 178 people on the plane be merely collateral damage?

Where do people get the idea that God works this way?

Through the years I have had hundreds of conversations with parents who've experienced the death of a child. A mother once said to me, "I thought that if I was a good person and pleased God, then nothing bad would ever happen to me. But now the worst possible thing has happened, and I'm afraid I'm losing my faith. Either God is angry at me, or what I've been taught about God is all wrong."

My response was to reflect the question back to her and ask, "Which do *you* think it is? Which one of those options feels more like truth to you?" Is God angry at you, or is your concept of God simply evolving?"

If one's faith is defined by a belief that God rewards us for piousness by protecting us from harm, then that faith will certainly be challenged when harm occurs. And harm, in one form or another, *will* occur, it's guaranteed. The biggest lie we have ever been told is that faith in God – *any god* – can protect us from experiencing trauma or loss. A crisis of faith, especially if our faith is based on what we've been told rather than what we've experienced via personal revelation, can lead us toward a whole new way of seeing the world, and a chance to turn the corner on Grief Street.

A mother who had recently lost her nine year-old son to leukemia told me, "When I was five years old, I was playing too rough with a kitten and accidentally broke its neck and killed it. And when I was 22 I had an abortion. I often wonder if God is punishing me for these things by taking my son."

And another mother once said to me, "I spend all my time wondering what I did wrong and how I can correct it and be right with God so I can see my child again in Heaven."

It is heartbreaking to hear stories like this. Which god, exactly, are these women talking about? Although the women in these examples identified themselves as Christians, there is no doctrine of "tit-for-tat" punishment during physical life in Christian teachings. So where do these ideas come from?

God or Godzilla?

The fear-based view of God that many Christians embrace was personified in a legendary sermon by Christian theologian Jonathan Edwards in 1941 entitled, *Sinners in the Hands of an Angry God.* Edwards presented hell as a real, physical location, promised an eternity of punishment for all who do not embrace Christ, and specifically cited scripture that expresses God's wrath at the "wicked unbelieving Israelites" who deserve "infinite punishment" for their sins.[9]

The god described in these scenarios leads us not to grace, but to cognitive dissonance. On one hand he is a pillar of righteousness, love and virtue which humans are asked to revere and emulate, but he also appears to be equal part violent psychopath, prone to irrational rages, racial bigotry and mass murder. This god has mood swings that Princeton theologian Philip Helsel compares to bi-polar disorder,[10] and Helsel describes our attempts to understand or worship such a god as requiring a "sacrifice of the intellect."

If God is a psychopathic father, his children have no choice but to cower in fear of his wrath and unpredictable outbursts. God as a father figure is a popular anthropocentric idea, as evidenced by the many parents who use the threat "God will punish you" as a way to keep children in line. Researchers Hart Nelsen and Alice Kroliczak quote a 1964 study of parents who used this tactic to present themselves as part of a special coalition with God in order to control children's behavior. The study observed that this strategy was used primarily by low income, less educated parents who had sect-like religious preferences.[11]

In her 2011 article, *A Beautiful Anger*, Christian writer Linda Falter states that the terrifying aspects of God's behavior are in fact part of God's nature, along with his other human attributes, such as eyes and bowels. She even compares God's actions to her own actions as a parent, and wonders why humans created a god with a parental type of personality. But rather than follow this questioning with psychological insight and an educated approach to research, she simply concludes that God's behavior is "beyond our pay grade to judge," since God's anger is different than ours because it has a "holier purpose."[12]

These are examples of unquestioning, obedient allegiance to the anthropomorphized God in which so many Westerners believe. Rather than analyzing the behavior of the mythical entity written about by the ancients and identifying the reasons why that entity's behavior so accurately reflects our own, Ms. Falter, like millions of other believers, simply shrugs it off as a mystery that we are not worthy to comprehend. And here we find the core of a deep theological question... how could God's anger be different than our own if *we created* the idea of an angry God in the first place?

In David Lamb's article *God Behaving Badly*, he defends the violent, random behavior of the angry god by defining it as an "effective means of reducing violent crime and promoting peace among his people."[13] But even if there is reasonable cause for creating a god who punishes people in these ways, the problems occur when people believe that the stories about God's wrath are *historical fact.*

Literal interpretation of stories where God wants us to beat our children with rods (Proverbs 23:13-14), threatens to kill someone for letting their hair become unkempt (Leviticus 10:6) or kills an entire tribe of people but saves the virgin girls for the soldiers (Numbers 31:17) are just a few examples (of hundreds) in which God behaves like an urban crime lord rather than the benevolent lord of the universe. No wonder we can't make sense of anything that happens to us. With this view of God, we are firmly planted on a foundation based on fear and separation instead of a path to higher understanding, peace and unity. When we approach God from an innate sense of inadequacy and self-loathing rather than personal empowerment, then the experience of grief and loss will inevitably be colored by guilt, fear and helplessness.

Many of the world's leading religious scholars, such as John Dominic Crossan, Tom Harpur, Richard Elliott Friedman and Bart Ehrman have devoted their lives to pointing out the distinction between myth and reality in Judeo-Christian literature. Crossan makes a definitive statement when he says, "It is not that those ancient people told literal stories and we are now smart enough to take them symbolically, but that they told symbolic stories that we are now dumb enough to take literally."[14] And as Harpur astutely points out, literalism deprives us of the deeper meanings in these stories by providing a one-dimensional view of concepts that have the potential for multiple levels of understanding... *if they are interpreted symbolically.*

Typical of this one-dimensional view is the idea of a god that demands flawless compliance and responds with violent, catastrophic retribution whenever his demands are not met. The creation of this divine "personality" was possibly the result of the Jewish mindset during the Babylonian exile when the Pentateuch was finally written down after 1000 years of oral transmission. The god described by the writers mirrored the behavior of their cruel, tyrannical oppressors.

One popular conservative Christian view sees human experience as divided into a dualistic universe containing only God (good) and the Devil (evil), and teaches that all good experience comes from God and all bad experience comes from the Devil. In this view, since trauma and pain do not come from God, they have no purpose other than to support the agenda of the Devil. Pain and trauma should be avoided, and if they do occur, it's seen as some sort of great cosmic error, as frequently expressed by many grievers who lost their loved ones "before their time." Although this type of belief in Satan may be extreme, it permeates Western culture in more ways than we realize. According to Christian evangelical minister Patrick Kelly, "Suffering is an instrument of Satan... It is Satan who wants to see the drug addict use, the alcoholic drink, the weak fall down, and the ego-filled self implode... it is not God's will that anyone should suffer."[15]

But from a less dogmatic perspective, the "implosion of the ego-filled self" is actually a goal to which one might aspire rather than an experience to be avoided. Kelly's description of suffering suggests that breaking down the ego is the evil work of Satan, which implies that God *wants* us to live in the ego and that there is no wisdom to be gained from our traumatic experiences. In this view, if suffering is not part of God's will, then negative experience has no purpose. This belief suggests that if we are good Christians (according to Kelly), we should be spared from all suffering and therefore live in a static condition where there are no emotional, intellectual or spiritual challenges. Perhaps this idea is deeply rooted in the minds of the bereaved parents who expressed their views earlier in this chapter.

At the other end of the spectrum we find the teachings of Buddhism, in which egolessness *is* the goal, and we can work with suffering to help us understand how loss and impermanence can be paths to awakening. Buddhist nun, teacher and author Pema Chodron says, "We always want to get rid of misery rather than see how it works with joy... Inspiration and wretchedness complement each other...With only inspiration we become arrogant. With only wretchedness, we lose our vision." [16]

Moving From Pain to Peace

As Pema says, inspiration and wretchedness are both necessary for a balanced human experience. Pain, fear, loss and tragedy are very clear moments that shock us out of complacency into a more flexible state in which we can shift and grow if we're willing to allow our religious and cultural definitions to be transformed. Four of Chodron's key points stand out as the most enlightened view of tragedy I have ever heard:

1. We use painful situations to wake us up rather than put us to sleep

This means that we can choose to become angry and bitter, to shut people out, to feel victimized and to live a disconnected life ruled by fear. That would be sleep. Or we could learn to notice all the miraculous events that occur around the edges of any painful experience and realize that these events are roadmaps leading us to new possibilities. Taking it one step further, it is, in fact, our own intention, our own higher selves or souls or God, whatever we choose to call it, that brought forth the painful situation and created its gifts in the first place.

2. We invite in what we would usually try to avoid
When faced with intense pain, we instinctively recoil from it, saying, "please make this go away, I'm not ready for this, I don't want this." Imagine that instead of resisting, we said instead, "OK, I will receive this. What's in this that I need to know? Let it come, I will accept, and I will follow this path with openness and trust."

3. We realize that only to the extent to which we expose ourselves to annihilation, can that which is indestructible be found in us.
The more vulnerable we are, the more we are willing to risk, the more information and guidance we will receive, and the faster change and expansion will manifest.

4. We learn that bad news, pain, fear, loss and tragedy are actually very clear moments that teach us to lean in and feel rather than to back away from feeling and experiencing. And in that sense, tragedy can be seen as good news, not bad.
Lean in! What a beautiful expression. To lean in to pain rather than to pull away from it looks something like this... you're diagnosed with cancer, your 14 year-old daughter is pregnant, you've lost all your money in the stock market and you lose your job. You've tried everything you can to change these circumstances, but it isn't working. Do you kick and scream and resist and fight and rage and vent and blame? Sure you do... for a while. And then you wake up and deal with it. You lean into it and ask it to engulf you. You receive it in its entirety. And you find that it leads you to a whole set of astonishing new possibilities that you might not have ever imagined. You lean in to even the worst imaginable scenario, and you ultimately are

led to that place of fearlessness and egolessness, because the worst imaginable thing has already happened. Where else is there to go? The alternative is helplessness, powerlessness and victimhood.

Pema Chodron brings us a Buddhist perspective, but these are not uniquely Buddhist concepts. Catholic theologian Richard Rohr shares similar ideas from a Christian vantage point in his article *Complaining to God,*[17] which addresses grief specifically as it relates to men and their difficulties expressing emotion. He points out that although one third of the Psalms are "lamentations" (a form of prayer in which we complain to God about our suffering), these psalms are rarely used in Catholic and Protestant liturgies. Rohr thinks these prayers are viewed as expressing a "sinful" anger or negativity, when in fact, the free expression of grief is something quite different. He states, "We think they [the lamentations] make us appear weak, helpless, and vulnerable, and most of us don't want to go there. We think, perhaps, they show a lack of faith, whereas they are probably the summit of faith."

Rohr quotes Robert Bly's observation that "grief work is the privileged and powerful entrance way for most men out of their controlling heads and finally into their bodies and hearts," but I would add that this is true for all of us, male and female. Without an awareness of the gifts of grief, as Rohr describes, "our pain, sadness, and tragedies are not teaching us, but only deafening us and blinding us. And they are our greatest teachers, even though we are never quite sure what it is that they have taught us."

As free-thinking human beings, we have a choice as to how we perceive an experience or event. Bereaved parent Mark Ireland wrote about his young son's death in his book, *Soul Shift,* "I could feed it my grief and pain or I could feed it my wonder and faith. Once I changed my outlook, I realized that my loss was not a meaningless accident. I woke up to a greater potential and gained a reference point from which I could contribute to the universe in new ways."[18]

Ireland's statement exemplifies what grief expert John Archer defines as a "redefinition of attachment" in response to grief.[19] The truth is that we never, *ever* have to detach from our departed loved ones, nor do we have to completely "let go" of them. We simply have to redefine what attachment means and what the relationship looks like. It is the dreadful expectation of detachment – *letting go* – that keeps so many bereaved individuals from finding peace, and this expectation is constantly reinforced by well-meaning friends and even professional counselors who are not specifically trained in grief work. By contrast, as Ireland so eloquently explained, we can choose to shift the meaning and the character of our attachment. If we can do that with our attachments to loved ones who have died, then we can also do it with our attachments to beliefs about how the universe is supposed to work.

When faced with loss and grief, we find ourselves at a crossroads where there are unlimited options, including a bitter rejection of spirituality. But rather than disconnecting from spiritual life entirely, we can allow the life-altering event to integrate with our personalities, alter our perspectives and help us to focus less on *what* happened and more on how we can *work with* what happened.

Rabbi David Cooper, a brilliant contemporary mystic often referred to as "The Buddhist Rabbi," describes God as a *process* rather than a *being*. In this view, we are part of the energetic creative force of the universe, functioning as co-creators rather than children of a father. If we see God as a father, we relinquish all our power as co-creators, or, as Cooper says, "As long as we relate to God as Father and we as children, we sustain the dysfunctional paternalistic model in which Father knows best. We not only remain alienated with a sense of abandonment, we relinquish our personal sense of responsibility."[20]

A self-empowered form of spirituality in which God is not a protector/punisher/father but is simply the creative force from which we emanate, allows us to see that this force actually works in *partnership* with us rather than scrutinizing and supervising us. If we see God as a partner rather than a parent, we begin to see ourselves as equal parts of a collective energy that IS God rather than aspects of creation that inhabit a location separate from God. In our role as co-creators, there is a reason and a purpose for every experience. Illness, loss, trauma and death are not experiences to be avoided, but to be embraced with gratitude for the shifting of perceptions and gifts of growth they provide. Those who see God as a protector/punisher may feel betrayed, cheated or victimized by a traumatic experience, while someone with the co-creator perspective might see the same experience as a way to become more aligned with divine order.

When we can see the usefulness of a balanced life in which both the good and bad experiences have a proper and necessary place, we see that there is much to be grateful for, the so-called good with the so-called bad. All of it can be recognized for the sacred value of the journey, without judgment, without fear, and without seeing ourselves as doomed puppets being manipulated by frightening forces that we can't understand. This is a path to the true meaning of forgiveness, grace and unconditional love.

And therein lies the gift. Because when an experience cuts to the core of everything that defines us, we are forced out of our spiritual lethargy, and an opening is created that is highly receptive to growth. If we nurture that opening, if we honor it and work with it, we can discover previously unimagined worlds of peace and wisdom, and we can choose enlightenment over annihilation.

A New Story

Imagine how different we might feel if we were raised to interpret these Biblical stories in a metaphoric or symbolic way. Religious scholar Steven Hairfield imagined this, and put his findings into an extraordinary book called *A Metaphysical Interpretation of the Bible*. One of his brilliant interpretations sees the Exodus as an allegory or parable to teach about the journey of the soul during incarnation. We come to earth in a state of spiritual "enslavement" because as divine beings and eternal spirits, we are confined to the boundaries of a physical body and all the chaos and struggle that comes with it. We spend 40 years trying to find our way out of that slavery (40 years would have been a typical lifespan at the time), wandering around lost, seeking our way "home" to the Promised Land, i.e., to reunion with knowledge of our divine selves... our spiritual home.

Hairfield sees all the major Bible stories as mythical lessons, and says, "The Bible provides a guidebook for the journey of the soul as it moves from incarnation to incarnation... the path of experience that returns us to Source, or God." According to Hairfield, even the genealogical listings are more than just names. They are markers of our evolution and development as we become rooted in physical reality. Similarly, the Garden of Eden is emblematic of our arrival into the physical world, and expulsion from the garden represents the painful sense of separation and loss that comes with believing that physical reality is the *only* reality, and in so believing, we live in a state of separation, no longer one with Source/God.[21]

In a similar way, hospital chaplain Dennis Klipper uses the Exodus story as a way to help his substance abuse recovery patients by presenting it as a parable for attaining freedom from addiction. He explains that in every generation, in every struggle, we must see ourselves as having emerged from a figurative Egypt. Thus, the process of liberation referred to in the Exodus story becomes not only relevant in today's world, but can be applied specifically to the recovering patients.[22]

Klipper and Harifield are really on to something here. Seeing such stories as tools for guiding ourselves out of whatever psychic, spiritual or emotional enslavement we're dealing with at any moment allows us to use the stories as roadmaps that will help us move through our spiritual evolution. In a sense, we are all recovering patients, and this is particularly true for those who are struggling with acute or chronic grief.

I recently received an email from a woman – I'll call her Katie – who was upset by some of the rituals that took place at the funeral of her 90 year-old mother (the funeral was organized by her fundamentalist Christian siblings). At one point the minister covered the casket with a shroud to represent her mother's body being bathed in the blood of Christ as a way to guarantee entrance to Heaven. Katie found this particularly disturbing. She had abandoned the religion of her childhood decades earlier, and believed in reincarnation and a non-judgmental God. The death of their mother triggered a lot of conflict between Katie and her siblings, and she struggled heroically to keep her beliefs "in the closet" in order to keep peace. But this particular funeral ritual pushed her over the edge. Why did her mother need to be bathed in the blood of Christ? Couldn't she go to heaven without it?

I hear from hundreds of people who struggle with similar issues, and I have learned, through my own struggle, that the only way to find peace with this is to look for the common threads rather than the differences in religious beliefs and practices. The more I study theology, the more I see these threads, but it requires a very serious study that most people aren't willing to undertake.

What you'll find, if you're willing to take the time to look for it, is that the differences in religious doctrines are mostly due to semantics. The fact is that they're all talking about the exact same thing, and this becomes really apparent when you look at religious teachings using the "historical/critical method," which means taking into account all the elements that contributed to the establishment of those doctrines (historical setting, cultural influences, the intention of the writers, nuances in language, the political climate of the time, translations, interpretations, etc.). When all that is cleared away, we find amazing consistency from one tradition to another on the mystical level (as opposed to the socio-political level).

The mystics, whether Christian, Hindu, Jewish or Muslim, are all connecting to the same "god," and are receiving the same information. You can see this remarkable consistency in almost all of the mystical and channeled writings, from the ancient prophets and sages to today's contemporary mystics. This is because the channelers are receiving information directly from Spirit, without those other influences and narratives mucking up the true message. Once we understand this, disturbing rituals like the one Katie described are no longer disturbing, because we can interpret them symbolically. A cloth over a body to "bathe it in the blood of Christ" is no different than placing a "journey blanket" over a body the way a Native American family might, or the unadorned white shroud used in the Jewish tradition to show that all people are equal before God. It's all the same. It's all *symbolic.*

Religious myths are created to explain the natural and supernatural worlds, and to help us make sense of our experiences on earth. They are intended to express concepts that cannot be easily expressed in everyday language, but they are not intended to be *worshipped.* Looking at scripture as metaphor should in no way shake one's faith, but can actually *enhance* faith by giving it more meaning through teachings that can be understood and used in practical application.

And this is critically important for the bereaved.

NOTES

[16] Edwards, Jonathan. "Sinners in the Hands of an Angry God." *Internet Christian Library*.

[17] Helsel, Philip. "God Diagnosed with Bipolar I." *Pastoral Psychology* 58.2 (2009): 183-91.

[18] Nelsen, Hart M., and Alice Kroliczak. "Parental Use Of The Threat "God Will Punish": Replication and Extension." *Journal For The Scientific Study Of Religion* 23.3 (1984): 267-277.

[19] Falter, Linda. "A Beautiful Anger." *Christianity Today* 55.4 (2011): 34-6. Print.

[20] "God Behaving Badly." *Christianity Today* 55.7 (2011): 72-. Print.

[21] Harpur, Tom. *The Pagan Christ: Recovering the Lost Light*. New York: Walker &, 2005.

[22] Kelley, Patrick. Are Trauma, Tragedy, And Misfortune A Test Of Faith And Obedience? 2009. Shepherd's Care Ministries, Tucson, AZ. 27 Apr. 2010. www.findthepower.com/PageOne/SiteStartQuestionsTraumaAdversityAsATestof Faith.htm

[23] Chodron, Pema. When Things Fall Apart. Boston, MA: Shambala, 2000.

[24] Rohr, Richard. "Complaining to God by Richard Rohr, OFM." *Complaining to God by Richard Rohr, OFM*. N.p.29 Apr. 2011. <www.malespirituality.org/complaining_to_god.htm>.

[25] Ireland, Mark. (2008). *Soul Shift: Finding Where the Dead Go*. Berkeley, CA: Frog Books.

[26] Archer, 2002, 117. http://human-nature.com/nibbs/02/archer.html

[27] Cooper, David A. God Is a Verb: Kabbalah and the Practice of Mystical Judaism. New York. Riverhead, 1997. Print. P. 73

[28] Hairfield, Steven. *A Metaphysical Interpretation of the Bible*. Yakima, WA: Inner Circle Publishing, 2006.

[29] Klipper, Daniel S. "Use of the Exodus story with chemically dependent patients." *Chaplaincy Today* 21.1 (2005): 30-32.

5. Walking Point: Stories from the Trenches

"All is well, all is well.
Though everything is a mess, all is well."
Anthony DeMello

Wikipedia defines the term *walking point* as "assuming the first and most exposed position in a combat formation while advancing through hostile or unsecured territory." I love this term, and although it is generally used in a military context, I think it applies beautifully to the grief journey. For most of us, facing death – our own or another's – could easily be seen as unsecured or hostile territory, yet we must walk through it as fearlessly as possible.

Over the years I have had the privilege of helping thousands of individuals face death and grief. I have met some remarkable human beings and marveled at their ability to walk point through uncharted territory to find healing through a shift in spiritual perspective. I have also met many who were paralyzed with fear, anger and a need for blame, who were unable to take even one step toward acceptance.

In this chapter I'll share some of their stories, many of which sharply contrast with one another and give us a clear picture of the many possible addresses one might have on Grief Street:

Walking Bravely Toward Death

About a year ago I had the honor of working with a hospice patient named Walter. He was 70 years old and suffered from numerous medical problems, including ALS. Walter could not speak, but he was able to use his hands well enough to write on a little notepad. He was one of the sweetest, happiest human beings I have ever met. He was full of joy, and would often clap his hands gleefully or give a thumbs-up with a huge smile when he wanted to express his appreciation about something. I don't know if he'd been this way his entire life, or if he was simply happy because he knew his life would soon be over, but there was no question that he was looking forward to death. Sometimes he'd write on his little notepad, "I want to be dead." He'd hand me the message, and when I'd repeat it back to him, he'd give me a big smile and clap his hands. Once he wrote, "I want problems to weaken me and let me die. No scary pain."

Walter knew exactly what he wanted, and his family, friends and care team understood him perfectly. He didn't want medical intervention. He didn't want to experience pain or fear. He didn't want to be saved from death. I was not present the day he died, but I heard it was peaceful and beautiful (of course it was). I can still feel his joy and his radiant smile.

Another remarkable hospice patient with ALS was Doreen, a woman in her early 70s who made a conscious decision to allow death rather than continue living in a debilitated state that would burden her husband with caregiving. She was in the early stages of the disease and was relatively functional, but she knew what the future would look like, and her husband, who had health issues of his own, would not be able to care for her. She had recently lost her ability to swallow and was not able to eat, but rejected the idea of a feeding tube, choosing to listen to her body's signals and allow herself die naturally. She also opted to stop drinking water, knowing that without food and water, death would come sooner.

Doreen and I became very close during her days in hospice care. She talked to me at length about her life and her choice to die consciously. Sometimes I'd guide her through a special meditation in which I'd ask her to visualize a starry sky and imagine that she was inhaling the starlight with every breath, filling herself with the light of divine love, and exhaling any fear or pain that might be present. She loved doing this, and it always brought her tremendous peace.

Whenever I'd leave after one of our visits, we had a little code for saying goodbye. I'd say, "If I don't see you again in this world..." and she'd finish the sentence with, "I'll see you in the next!"

One day when I came to visit, Doreen told me about a dream she had in which an angel came into her room and put tiny stars on her tongue, "like tiny star-shaped pills." The angel said to her, "All you have to do is swallow these stars and you'll go to Heaven."

And the next day, she did.

The Native Way

I have many stories like this to share, but by far, the most eye-opening experience I've had with grief in a clinical setting was in December 2012. It was during a chaplaincy internship at a hospital, and I was called to the ICU to assist a Native American family that had just made the decision to remove their 72 year-old grandmother from life support.

When I arrived at the ICU, I was deeply moved by what I saw. There were about 20 family members of all ages around her bed, including young children. They had drums and rattles, and they were chanting Native prayers. In between songs and chants, they would cry and wail loudly. This is not something one sees very often in an urban hospital, and I was grateful and honored to have been invited into their circle.

I was told that some of the family members were Christians (Pentecostal), and they wanted me to offer Christian prayers and read bible passages, which I gladly did (it is not uncommon for Native American groups or individuals to combine another faith into their spiritual practice[23]). In addition to the requested Bible readings, I also offered my own prayers and blessings of love and honor for the grandmother, and often these prayers were spoken on top of the drumming and chanting in what could best be described as an exquisite spiritual song of unity in Spirit. In many ways, I felt like an outsider, so I asked the family if they wanted me to stay or leave, and they asked me to stay, which for me, was a sacred privilege.

But the most striking aspect of this was that these folks were sobbing and weeping *loudly*, blending their wailing with their singing. They expressed their grief freely, because they understood that the grief itself is a prayer. And I cried too, right along with them. Most of the time I simply stood there holding silent, scared space for them, tears streaming down my face as I basked in the conduit that had been opened to the spirit world by their free, unfettered expression of emotion.

It was a very holy experience. Not only were their hearts wide open, but they honored their family ties and spiritual traditions by taking the body home with them to bury on the family farm. It took a few hours to deal with the legal red tape, but arrangements were made for them to transport the body. When I saw them later as they were getting ready to leave the hospital, the kids were laughing and playing, the adults were talking and joking, and the energy around them was *luminous.* They had blown through all that intense pain in one big WHOOSH, letting it move through them as one unified energetic body. The pain of being without the grandmother's physical presence was not gone, and she would be missed, but the pain was now *processed,* through ritual, through appropriate directing of emotional energy and through acceptance of the soul's journey.

Walking Not-so-Bravely Toward Death

In contrast to this event, the next night at the hospital I was present for the death of an 86 year-old man who been in ICU for two days. He had already been resuscitated twice, but on the third attempt the doctors could not restart his heart. His wife and two adult sons were present, one of whom shouted demands at the nurses, snapped at his mother and younger brother, and dominated the scene with his anger. The wife was meek and mostly silent, dabbing her eyes delicately with a tissue at occasional tears while the younger son spent most of his time glowering at his older brother, his eyes filled with tears that were not allowed to fall. The only person expressing strong emotion was the angry brother.

Since they had requested the presence of a chaplain, I arrived on the scene and attempted to create an opening for the silent ones to talk about their feelings, but their stoicism was impenetrable. When I asked if they had any spiritual beliefs or practices that bring them comfort, the mother told me that they had no spiritual beliefs and would not be having a memorial service of any kind. I learned a few days later that this family planned to sue the hospital over a frivolous misunderstanding concerning the family's choice of a funeral home.

In these two stories, one family feels and expresses its pain fully, and the other suppresses it and projects it outward by looking for someone to blame. It could be said that these are two faces of grief… an idea that is eloquently explained in the following quote from Dr. Judith Johnson:

"If one person believes that death is bad and shouldn't happen, and the other accepts death as a normal part of the human journey, then who is likely to suffer more when grieving the death of a loved one? Clearly, the one who thinks death is bad and wrong. When something is unacceptable to us, we are so busy being angry and resistant to its reality that processing it and dealing with it are overwhelming. When someone accepts death, they can get on with the business of grieving their loss, while those unable to accept death must deal with their negative emotions about its existence as well. Accepting death is not about liking it, but acknowledging its normalcy and inescapable nature in the course of human life. Acceptance allows us to access the wisdom and intimacy with our loved ones that is available when we are not busy denying death." [24]

I once worked with a woman named Barbara whose 45 year-old son Jason was dying of pancreatic cancer. He'd lived a difficult life and there were many troublesome issues in the family dynamic, but now, after fighting the cancer for months, he had come home to his mother's farmhouse so she could care for him.

Barbara wanted desperately to help her son, but she could not bear to see him suffer, and tended to be emotionally overwrought and panicky around him. She was also terrified of death, and was not willing to consider hospice care (where Jason could be more comfortable and she could get some respite and emotional support), because she didn't think Jason was ready to die. When I asked what Jason 's doctors had to say, she told me that they never gave complete or comprehensible answers to her questions (though I suspect they *did* give her honest answers, and she wasn't able to hear them). I never actually met Jason, but it seems that he too was in denial about his impending death. Barbara often told me how the two of them would make plans to go fishing, take a trip to visit family in Canada and remodel the kitchen when he got better.

Jason did not get better, and he died alone on the bathroom floor in the middle of the night. When Barbara discovered his lifeless body, she became hysterical, threw a blanket over him (because she didn't want to look at him) and ran screaming into the living room, where she called 911.

Unlike millions of people whose loved ones die suddenly in car crashes, suicides, wars, murders or natural disasters, Barbara had a choice about how to cope with Jason's illness and death. She had the gift of time, and the opportunity to seek help. She had many options. But she would not agree to let me facilitate a conversation between her and Jason in which they could discuss the very real possibility of his death. Instead, she held on to the belief that he would miraculously recover and fed that illusion by fantasizing about fishing trips and home improvement projects. She would not consider hospice care, even though hospice could have helped her and Jason to talk about death and prepare for it. During the time I knew Barbara, I was never clear about whether or not Jason's doctor had suggested hospice as an option (he would have been seriously remiss if he hadn't, though some doctors encourage patients to "fight" until then end without ever offering hospice as an option).

Barbara was completely unprepared to deal with Jason's death. She had no tools, no rituals and no viable support. In the end, she was not even able to say goodbye. Jason's friends arranged a memorial service for him, but Barbara refused to attend.

For most of us, it is inconceivable that someone could respond to the death of a beloved friend, partner or child this way, but it is far more common than you might imagine. I remember Marnie, a woman I found crying in the waiting room of the in-patient hospice where I volunteered last year. I sat down and talked with her, and she was eager to tell me the story about how she and her husband Jack had tried every homeopathic remedy imaginable for his cancer, but he continued to decline, and now he was a hospice patient. I had not met Jack at this point, so I only had Marnie's side of the story to help me piece together a picture of their situation.

She said, "Jack keeps saying that he just wants this to be over, and then he asks what the plan is. I don't know what he means, so I tell him that the plan is for him to get better and come home."

I asked her, "If you could really listen to your heart for just a moment, and put your fear aside, what would you *think* he means?

And she said, "I don't know. I really don't know what he means."

"Well, perhaps you could ask him. Have you ever had an open, honest conversation about the various possible outcomes?"

"I know he's talking about death. He's been suffering for years, but I can't talk to him about it. I don't want to be the one to bring it up, because I don't want him to think I'm giving up on him. And he's not being direct about it because he doesn't want to upset me. And besides, I have confidence that he'll stabilize and he'll come home. He's only 71! He has a lot of years ahead of him."

We talked a bit more, and I told her that this would probably be a good time to push through that resistance and have a conversation about the very real possibility of death, which would be a relief to both of them and might provide the plan he's looking for. I told her that I could arrange for the chaplain or one of the social workers to visit the next day to help facilitate that conversation.

When we finished talking I went into Jack's room for the first time. The man I saw in the bed was very close to death. He must have weighed about 80 pounds and was barely conscious. I am not a nurse or doctor, but I've been around enough dying people to know when the end is near, and I wondered if the doctors, nurses, or social workers had talked to her about what to expect at this stage of the process. Based on my conversation with her, she was apparently not aware that he was actively dying. Had the staff not counseled her? Or *had* they, and she just wasn't able to hear it? The latter was far more likely.

My conversation with Marnie took place on Sunday, and Jack died on Tuesday. Thankfully, the chaplain met with them on Monday, but told me later that all he was able to do was advise Marnie to go with her gut instinct about how and when to talk with Jack about death.

How Some Grief Groups and Counselors Do More Harm than Good

Those of you who know me either personally or professionally will know that I have spoken out against some of the national grief groups for parents who've experienced the death of a child. One group in particular, which I will refer to as "Group X" has chapters all over the world, and a very strong online presence. The chapters and the online chat forums for this group are facilitated primarily by average folks whose only qualification as leaders is that they've lost a child. While there may be a few rare exceptions, these leaders have no training for their positions, and have no specific skills in counseling, active listening or spiritual care. They don't appear to be screened for religious bias or taught how to be accepting and non-judgmental in a public forum where participants represent a vast spectrum of diverse belief systems. In any other kind of counseling setting or public support scenario, it would be unthinkable to let such people facilitate a group in which vulnerable individuals are sharing their feelings and seeking help.

When I first began writing and teaching about death and the afterlife, I reached out to Group X because I knew that many of its members would benefit from the material I was sharing. But I was shocked to discover that my message about learning to perceive death and loss in a new way would be bitterly rejected by the group's national leadership (some of the angry comments found in Chapter Three are from members of Group X).

The group has a general policy at the national level (there are a few exceptions in individual chapters) to reject all discussion of spirituality, mediumship, near-death experience, deathbed visions and after-death communication, and will not allow presenters to address these topics at its annual conference. In keeping with this restriction, Group X closely monitors its Facebook page and routinely deletes any posts that appear on these subjects. I – along with several others of like mind – have been banned from posting on these pages because we tried to talk about these taboo topics. I once posted something about near-death experiences, and the group administrator replied with, "We are not to discuss religion on this page. Group X has a policy that we must remain *religiously neutral.*"

When I pointed out that NDEs have nothing to do with religion and my post didn't mention religion or spirituality of any kind, I was curtly told that I had no right to "tell people what to think and what to do." When I tried to respond, I found that my posting privileges in the group had been suspended and the conversation deleted.

But here's the kicker... after being so rudely dismissed from the group, I decided to read through some of the past postings, and saw dozens of posts about Jesus, heaven, dead people "earning their angel wings," God and prayer, including promotions for a Christian radio show and comments about Jesus dying on the cross for our sins.

So much for remaining "religiously neutral." And hence my point about the lack of training and facilitation skills among the group's leaders. When this sort of bias is present at the national level – particularly at the group's national conference – it represents not just an aversion to metaphysics and spirituality, but an aversion to offering healing tools that can actually help people.

I am part of a large group of teachers, counselors and bereaved individuals who feel that these groups – and any form of counseling that is not based in a thorough understanding of trauma, the grief process and the many diverse and varied pathways to healing – can actually inhibit people from moving forward over time.

Here are some stories from bereaved people who've experienced this first hand, with grief groups *and* private counselors:

Lori:

I went to a local meeting of Group X eight months after my ten year-old son died after a long battle with cancer. Prior to that, my husband and I had escaped our world for three months on a trip around the world, but when we returned home to an empty house without our son, we realized all we had done was prolong facing the harsh truth of his absence. The reentry was very difficult. I was barely hanging on and desperate for help so decided to attend this group meeting.

What I found there were many, many stories of grief and pain. There were poster boards filled with pictures of all the beautiful children who had died, and as I listened to the stories told by the parents, instead of feeling encouraged or hopeful that my pain would eventually become more manageable, I was actually taking on their pain, adding it to the burden of my own fragile state. Listening to these parents, some of whose children had died years before only carried me deeper into the abyss. Looking at them as examples of where I might be a few years from now was very discouraging.

The group organizers told me that it takes more than one meeting to really experience the benefits of the group, but my initial experience was so devastating that I never went back. There was no real help being offered... just the telling and re-telling of stories and the sharing of pain. While I know this has some benefit to healing in the early stages of grief, I could not see myself five years from now telling my story again and again. There had to be someplace to go from there.

Veronica:

My son hung himself on Mother's Day 2002 after speaking on the phone and telling me how much he loved me. About two weeks later, my sister and I decided to attend a meeting of Group X, because there was nothing in my area that addressed suicide specifically. My sister was the one who found my son, so she and I stuck close to each other for support.

But after one meeting we decided not to attend any more. We both couldn't help but notice that the majority of the group consisted of people who had lost their loved ones many years prior, yet still seemed to be "attached" to their grief. We both had the same feeling, and did not plan on being held captive by grief for years to come. While the people there were very loving and genuine, I didn't want to spend the rest of my life getting those "you poor dear" looks from people, and that group was full of those looks.

My next step was to seek a therapist who supposedly specialized in grief and trauma. I live in a rural area so there weren't many to choose from, and the few that looked promising didn't have an opening for eight weeks. I finally found Dr. S, who had an opening in two weeks. At the very first session I was unsure that we were a good fit, but I kept hearing from family members that "you really need to see someone," so I gave him a chance.

In that session, he listened to my story and gave me a homework assignment. He wanted me to talk about my anger toward my son for what he had done, but I wasn't aware of feeling any anger (perhaps I did have anger but wasn't quite ready to acknowledge it). All I knew at the time was that I ached for my child, knowing that he was in so much pain that he chose to do this terrible thing to himself,

Dr. S insisted that I was burying anger toward my son and that it needed to be dug out ASAP (bear in mind this is only about a month after my son's death). He told me to write a letter to my son expressing my anger and bring it to the next appointment.

So I tried to write this letter, because he was the therapist and he knew what he was doing, right? But I struggled to come up with something, and the only thing I could say was "Gee Adam, why did you have to do it right upstairs from your auntie, right after smoking a cigarette with your younger cousin? What if *he* had been the one to find your body?" But I didn't really feel that way. I was just trying to do what the therapist asked of me. I figured I was supposed to be angry.

At my second session with Dr S, he asked me if I still cried and how often. I said I cry every day for my son. I can hold it together all day at work but as soon as I hit the parking lot, the flood gates open and I cry while driving home. He then decided to write me a prescription for anti-depressants. I said no, I don't think I am clinically depressed, I am just grieving. He said that it was not normal to cry every day, so I must be depressed. I reminded him that it had only been six weeks since my son hung himself (on Mother's Day), and I felt certain that at this stage it was OK to still cry every day. He spent the rest of the session trying to convince me to take the medication... at one point he asked me why I was so opposed to it, and I told him that I don't like to take any drugs if it's not absolutely necessary. Besides, I sensed it was important to FEEL what I was going through, and not numb it.

Eventually, I told him I didn't like the side effects of those meds, and that's when he said the most inappropriate and unprofessional thing imaginable. He said, "Yes, but those mostly affect men, not women." He held up his index finger straight and tall, and then let it flop over, indicating a flaccid penis. He was obviously referring to the sexual side effects of some anti-depressants, but at that point all I could do was stand up, say goodbye and walk out.

Candace

Shortly after my daughter's death I began to see a therapist for my grief. I selected this person based on the fact that she was the director of the institute where I had once studied and worked. "Dr. M" had studied with Elizabeth Kubler Ross and had some degree of fame for the books she'd published and her many TV appearances.

For the first few visits, things were handled professionally, but two weeks later, I did not get the usual day-before-appointment reminder call. Feeling certain that I had an appointment, I called first thing the following morning to confirm. The secretary informed me that there was no appointment on the books for me. Not sure of where we stood on things that we had discussed, I left a message for Dr. M to return my call. After a week, I had still not heard from her.

I had for months been experiencing that very odd feeling of things not being real, often felt in grief. The strange behavior of Dr. M not returning my calls only reinforced these feelings. "Perhaps I misunderstood," I thought to myself.

But this therapist who was supposed to be helping me cope with grief was treating me like a bad date she never wanted to see again. It was extremely awkward. Despite the awkwardness, I contacted her office again, this time via email. Her secretary responded by indicating that the doctor was "very busy" with her "other business" (which included directing an organization and promoting herself as an author and speaker). The secretary also revealed that Dr. M was dealing with an uncle who was dying from cancer.

How silly I felt! Certainly with such a tragedy, she had to attend to her family. I completely understood and went about my business with other things in my life. I was sure I would hear from her when things calmed down. But I didn't.

Two months later, I ran into an old friend who was familiar with Dr. M, and she informed me that Dr. M had a habit of sometimes "disappearing" for weeks, even months." I had never in my life heard of anyone conducting themselves like this with clients.

Several days later, I got a text message from Dr. M apologizing for not getting back with me. I replied, but she did not answer. Weeks went by and I did not hear from her. Dr. M baited me yet again, but then refused to communicate further. Astonishingly, later that evening, I received another text message from Dr. M that totally shocked me. It said, "Sorry I have not gotten back with you. My dog died. I was grieving."

Even though I knew that her behavior was indicative of who she was and it had nothing to do with me, my ego could not help but feel as if she mocked my grief. I could not help but feel that she intentionally indicated that the loss of her dog was equal to my loss. I also sensed that if she treated me this way, she probably treated her other clients in the same manner.

What if I had been deeply depressed, or suicidal? Her behavior could further traumatize someone who was suffering from the complications of PTSD along with grief. Fortunately, I was able to use the situation to motivate myself to urge others who seek counseling to see only a qualified grief therapist.

Perhaps There is a Better Way

I asked my friend Dr. Piero Parisetti,[25] a medical doctor who is also a trained psychotherapist and grief counselor, to help me with this chapter by contributing some information on alternative forms of grief therapy. Dr. Parisetti proposes a radical shift in grief counseling models that would incorporate mystical events such as mediumship readings, after-death communication, near-death experiences, deathbed visions and other phenomena that are commonly experienced by the dying and bereaved. Acknowledging these experiences can lead to the realization that there IS no death, and hence, the bereaved and the dying do not need to see the loss as absolute and permanent.

In a society that sees death through a fog of terror and superstition, it is no wonder that we have a long way to go in terms of addressing grief in a truly effective way. To add insult to injury, in 2013 the "bible" of the psychotherapy industry – *The Diagnostic and Statistical Manual of Mental Disorders* (DSM) – revoked its long-standing "bereavement exclusion." The exclusion made an exception for bereaved individuals who exhibited signs of depression, and stated that clinicians should not "diagnose major depressive disorder (MDD) after the recent death of a loved one... even when the patient met the usual MDD criteria."[26] But now that this exclusion no longer stands, a person *can* be diagnosed with Major Depressive Disorder and prescribed medication if they are not showing signs of recovery from a loss after two weeks. *Two weeks!* Instead of helping clinicians to better understand grief, this change essentially "medicalizes" or "pathologizes" the grief experience and suggests that it can be treated with medication.

What Dr. Parisetti proposes – as do many other bereavement experts who have reviewed the research on what Dr. Lou LaGrand calls "extraordinary experiences of the bereaved"-- is that we allow acknowledgment of these experiences to be part of the healing process.

Real Help for Grief
Contributed by
Piero Parisetti MD

The suffering caused by the death of a loved one ranks among the most distressing of human experiences. It is also, sadly, one of the most common. Just as each person is unique, each loss is unique and each individual's reaction to loss is unique. Medical research shows that there is no "right" or "wrong" way to cope with grief, and there are no "better" or "worse" persons in the face of such intense suffering.

Following a loss, most people experience what is defined as *normal grief* - a period of intense sorrow, numbness and even guilt or anger. While for many people these feelings gradually ease, for some, these feelings can be devastating and do not improve with the passage of time. This is called *complicated grief,* and it is a debilitating condition which requires professional attention.

But what kind of professional attention is most effective?

More and more medical and counseling professionals are learning that alternative approaches to grief counseling can be far more effective than traditional talk therapy. By "alternative," I am referring to an approach that openly admits the existence of an afterlife while remaining science-and-evidence-based. In the words of Dr Carl Wickland, director of the National Psychopatic Institute of Chicago:

"What becomes of the dead? This problem is of vital interest to the patient who lingers on the borderland of transition,

doubtful of the future, or perhaps trembling in fear of his probable condition after the tomorrow of death. Should it not be the noblest part of the physician's calling, in such situations, to be in a position to assure his patient from actual knowledge, that there is no death, but a birth into new fields of activity and opportunities in the higher mental spheres?"

Working with an understanding of the afterlife in therapy eliminates beating around the bush, politically correct attitudes and fear about opening up a theological can of worms. It's just a matter of gently helping the patient see that death as we commonly think of it DOES NOT EXIST. This is not a matter of faith or wishful thinking, but is based on compelling evidence from experts who have conducted bona fide scientific research on the survival of consciousness after death, and have used non-traditional approaches to help the dying and the bereaved process their grief.

These non-traditional approaches have three things in common:

a) They were introduced or investigated by scientists, medical doctors or mental health professionals.
b) They either imply or are based on the existence of an afterlife.
c) They are extraordinarily effective.

Unresolved grief is considered pathological in stage models (e.g. Kübler-Ross, 1969), and the goal of traditional psychotherapy sessions is to "work through the stages" and resolve the sense of loss. But the stage theory has received precious little experimental support. Research indicates that the stages of grief in fact do not necessarily exist. Dr Elizabeth Kubler-Ross herself, toward the end of her life, openly admitted that this was not a universally applicable model, and that she didn't think everybody had to go through the stages in sequence.

Nevertheless, as the model is simple, logical and appealing, it spread like a cholera epidemic, infecting the entire grief counseling profession and expanding into other areas of psychology and sociology.

In a 2007 paper[27], researchers Larson and Hoyst pointed to the popular yet pessimistic consensus in the grief and bereavement literature that grief counseling was at best ineffective, while at worst harmful to clients seeking help. Similarly, in a 2008 meta-analysis of traditional psychotherapeutic grief treatment outcomes,[28] Currier, Neimeyer and Berman revealed a "discouraging picture for bereavement interventions" which added "little to no benefit beyond the participants' existing resources and the passage of time."

We are seeing that traditional interventions are based on an unsupported theoretical model and do not seem to work. And still, this is what the overwhelming majority of grieving people are offered. The good news however, is that non-traditional interventions and experiences have been repeatedly demonstrated to dramatically diminish grief. Scientific research (the same science that often ridicules our claims about the afterlife) shows that approaches implying the existence of an afterlife *do* work.

What are These "Extraordinary Experiences?"

Spontaneous apparitions (visions) of the dead are commonly reported. Medical reports show that at least half of all persons whose spouse dies report a spontaneous contact from that person after death. Similar reports frequently come from parents who have lost a child, and this phenomenon is of great interest to those who work to alleviate the negative consequences of unresolved grief. Research indicates that people who have had an experience of after-death communication with a deceased loved one, either spontaneously, through a medium or with other techniques, show marked and lasting improvements in their psychological well-being.

In one example of "afterlife-based" grief counseling approaches, let's look at the work of clinical psychologist Dr. Allan Botkin. Dr. Botkin's method, which he calls *Induced After-Death Communication* (IADC), is an offshoot of the EMDR (eye movement desensitization and reprocessing) technique. EMDR was introduced by Dr. Francine Shapiro of California and is referred to by the World Health Organization – together with Cognitive Behavior Therapy - as "the only psychotherapies recommended for children, adolescents and adults with post-traumatic stress disorder."

While focusing on the therapist's hand, the patient is asked to move the eyes left or right rhythmically and focus on a disturbing thought, feeling, image, or sensation. In IADC therapy, the client who is disturbed by someone's death is asked to focus directly on their sadness during the eye movements. Amazingly, in a typical IADC session, the patients report having had the experience of a direct, real life encounter with the deceased person, and receiving evidential and comforting messages. In a number of cases, the deceased person relates information previously unknown to the client.

Skeptics refer to these experiences as "hallucinations," but the after-death communication experience is unanimously described as very different from hallucinations. Technically, hallucinations are perceptions that do not correspond to sensory input, which means that hallucinations are all in one's head and have nothing to do with any reality that exists separate from us. Hallucinations generally have a very negative content, vary considerably in content from person to person, and are thought to be a symptom of a severe psychological disorder. It is clear, however, that IADC content is uniformly positive, very consistent in content from person to person, and very healing psychologically.

Based on thousands of cases (Botkin trained his clinical psychology assistants in IADC therapy, and several dozen therapists now utilize it broadly around the world), Botkin offers this summary of 20 years of experience that he and his collaborators have had with this method:

"It doesn't matter what you believe, what we believe, or even what the experiencers believe. The IADC experiences we have induced in thousands of patients result in dramatic life changes that heal grief and trauma in a very short time and are sustained long-term... One conclusion is clear: the IADC induction procedure offers the means to alleviate a great amount of human suffering. There is no greater pain in life than losing a child, a battlefield buddy, or a spouse of many years and feeling disconnected forever. We lose a part of ourselves when we lose someone so important to us. But now, thanks to processes like IADC, we can routinely heal this deep pain, as well as anger, guilt, and the other emotions resulting from the loss."

The survival of consciousness and human personality beyond bodily death is obviously an extraordinary claim, and, as famously said by Carl Sagan, it requires extraordinary evidence. Contrary to popular belief, such evidence has been collected for 150 years by some of the brightest scientific minds on the planet, including four Nobel Prize winners. When examined with the care it deserves, this evidence leaves little doubt that the extraordinary claim of survival is in fact substantiated.

How Does Mediumship Help?

Another method that can promote healing from grief is very simple... a sitting with a gifted medium that obtains evidential proof that a deceased loved one continues to exist in a non-material dimension, which we call *the spirit world* (for lack of a better word).

Rather than focusing on scientific evidence, I prefer to talk about the *effects* that an evidential sitting with a medium has on the bereaved sitter. This is one of the areas investigated by *applied* psychical research. While fundamental psychical research is concerned with collecting evidence about extraordinary human experiences and developing theoretical models, *applied* psychical research investigates the practical applications of the phenomena.

In the case of medium sittings, researching the effects on the sitter may sound like investigating whether water is wet. After all, obtaining proof of the survival of a loved one is the very reason bereaved people seek out mediums in the first place. Anybody who has either personally experienced or witnessed after-death communication through a medium knows how effective this can be in reducing grief. Whether in the privacy of a one-to-one sitting, during a spiritualist church ceremony or even in one of the showbiz events we see on television, if the medium is good and provides good evidence, people experience major relief.

But sadly, these effects were never properly studied scientifically, and information was based solely on the self-evident reality of the sitters' personal experience. However, in 2007, studies began to emerge, beginning with work by Drs. Gary Schwartz and Julie Beischel at the University of Arizona in a triple blind study of mediums and sitters that effectively eliminated conventional mechanisms as explanations for the information reception.

Schwartz and Beischel concluded, "Certain mediums can anomalously receive accurate information about deceased individuals."[29] Later, in 2010, Julie Beischel and Mark Boccuzzi of the Windbridge Institute carried out another exploratory study using an anonymous survey methodology in which 83 participants were asked to retrospectively rate their levels of grief before and after a reading with a medium. As expected, results strongly indicated that participants experience meaningful reductions in levels of grief. But, in my view, the real value of the study lies in the fact that one third of participants also worked with a mental health professional and were able to draw comparisons between the two approaches.

Verbatim comments from the participants are extremely telling:

"The medium had a profound effect on my life and my grieving process... It has helped me in a way I never would have imagined."

"After the reading, I had a different definition of my relationship with my mom that was more special than I could ever expect."

"The medium helped me manage the grief that has been with me for more than 20 years."

"When my first MHP [mental health practitioner] negated the reading I had with a medium, I switched to someone who understood and supported 'my new reality' and received much more constructive help with my grief."

"I only went to a grief counselor for four sessions. I did not continue because I didn't feel that she was helping me either way."

"I know that I personally needed to go through counseling as well. However, the level of healing was accelerated by getting readings."

"The medium reached my heart, the social worker my mind."

The researchers also discussed the advantages of mediumship readings over the frequently reported spontaneous experiences of after-death communication. They concluded, "Readings may be less frightening, less intimidating and easier to understand than personal, spontaneous experiences. The scheduled and regulated environment of a reading makes it well-suited as a controlled and prescribable treatment option. A medium serves as a non-judgmental participant in the experience who will not disparage or pathologize the experiences of the bereaved."

With this information we are left once again to ponder over the tragic failures of traditional grief counseling approaches, and on the evident success of non-traditional approaches based on − or implying − the existence of an afterlife. Thoughts about the finality of death (one's own or a loved one's) fuel a large part of suffering for the dying and the bereaved. When these thoughts are shown − through knowledge and reason − to be unjustified, the suffering connected with them can be lifted. This, of course, will not transform bereavement into a day at the beach. Death and dying come with an unavoidable load of suffering that can't be avoided, because it is a basic human experience that we simply have to go through. But correcting the basic thought that "death=annihilation" can be powerfully healing.

By correcting the negative, unrealistic (in light of the evidence) thoughts about death, one can indeed transform the fear of death and heal the pain of bereavement.

When Religion Doesn't Help

The last thing I want to do is to come across as disrespectful for what are likely to be the most cherished, fundamental beliefs for many people around the world. I insist in saying that, although I am not religious myself, I greatly respect religions and, especially, religious people. Nevertheless, I cannot help but notice that many common religious beliefs about death and the afterlife are:

a) In sharp contrast with masses of evidence and testimony consistently coming to us from different lines of investigation.

b) Quite unhelpful for a person who is facing death or grieving the loss of a loved one.

A few years ago I had the painful experience of accompanying my dearest friend through a three-year dramatic battle with cancer. What was painful was *not* being at my friend's side during those difficult times... I actually consider that a very enriching experience. The painful part was that he died an anguished man. A committed Catholic, he was convinced that he was to face judgment for sins he believed he had committed.

At that time I already knew that we have no evidence whatsoever for this kind of judgment. All the testimony we have, from a diverse range of sources, consistently speaks of a "life review" instead of punishment. In this review, we are not "judged" by others, but are helped to make sense of the life we lived and to understand our life's purpose. We have not the tiniest shred of evidence in support of any sort of eternal hell or damnation. Instead, we are helped to learn, sometimes painfully, and then to progress.

Similar in many ways is the case of a neighbor, a lovely lady in her early 50s who looked 20 years older. For years she'd been grieving the premature death of her husband, which had taken a big toll on her mind and body. When I said that I knew things that perhaps could help relieve some of her grief, she listened to me politely for a while, but then said that she could not entertain the idea that consciousness survives death – and especially the idea of after death communication – because of her religious thinking.

This is *tragic.* If religions, as Karl Marx famously said, are people's opium, then they should make people feel good, or at least feel *less bad*. They should not add more confusion and suffering to the process of dying and grieving.

I am pretty convinced that if you were to ask ten Catholic or Christian people for a detailed description of what happens after we die, you would get ten different answers. Where do people go before resurrection? Does resurrection happen for everybody? Do bad people go to hell immediately, or after judgment day? Do you have to be first resurrected and then, if bad, go to hell? What happens if you are bad and repent? Where does purgatory lie in the sequence of events? I believe these ideas look absurd, inconsistent and incoherent even to many of the faithful, yet people cling to these beliefs with fervor. What is particularly sad is that for most grieving people, these beliefs provide more confusion than comfort.

I have seen many bereaved people suffer needlessly worrying that their loved ones did not go to heaven because they did not accept Jesus as their savoir or repent their sins. But doesn't God forgive *everybody?* If so, then why is repentance needed? This kind of circular thinking goes on forever and ends up nowhere. Let's focus for a moment on the belief that speaking with the dead is sinful. The main support for this belief is found in three verses from the book of Leviticus in the Hebrew Bible:

> *"Do not turn to mediums or necromancers; do not seek them out, and so make yourselves unclean by them: I am the Lord your God."*[30]

> *"A man or a woman who is a medium or a necromancer shall surely be put to death. They shall be stoned with stones; their blood shall be upon them."* [31]

> *"For these nations, which you are about to dispossess, listen to fortune-tellers and to diviners. But as for you, the Lord your God has not allowed you to do this."* [32]

These statements clearly prohibit consultations with the spirit world. If you accept Leviticus and Deuteronomy as the inerrant word of the Almighty, then you would be wise to avoid any contact with mediums. But before you make such a decision, you might want to know what else you are signing on for if you choose to abide by these ancient prohibitions.

Have you ever eaten a rare steak? Have you ever trimmed your hair or beard? Did you ever get a tattoo; peek at your brother in the nude; fail to stand when an old man enters the room? Have you ever worn a shirt of cotton and polyester blend? Perhaps you have cursed a politician or made fun of a bald man or worked on the Sabbath. According to the biblical laws, all these acts and many,

many others are sins against the Lord and are condemned just as strongly as consulting a medium.

Finally (and this is even more difficult to accept for Christians), most of what we know of Christianity has very little, if anything, to do with the teachings of Jesus. The earliest known gospel was written 50 years after his death, and as the "new religion" spread over the Roman Empire during the next 200 years, what we know today as "Christian doctrine" was established. It did NOT come from Jesus or from anybody who was an eyewitness to his ministry.

This is not a tirade against religion. It is a tirade against the unnecessary suffering deriving from uncritically accepting poorly understood religious teachings.

Evidence from psychical research points to an entirely different view about life and the afterlife. My advice is to consider the evidence, study it, reflect upon it. Use your intelligence, your reason, and draw your own conclusions from the data. Chances are, as medical research proves, you may emerge with a clearer – and extraordinarily more comforting – understanding of death and the afterlife.

Piero Parisetti MD,
Milan, Italy

The Next Frontier

I sincerely believe that the next frontier for social and spiritual transformation in our culture is the awareness and acceptance of death. And I'm honored to be part of the generation that's on the leading edge of this movement.

For the past 50 years the baby boom generation has been distinguished by its ability to break through social conventions. We directed the harsh light of truth onto the sexual repression, racism, religious dogma and blind patriotism that dominated the social landscape in the 1950s and 1960s, and we produced a crop of brilliant leaders who paved the way for transformation. Social activists like Gloria Steinem, Jesse Jackson and Tom Hayden;

spiritual teachers like Marianne Williamson, Ram Dass and Carolyn Myss; and media moguls like Oprah Winfrey have opened doors to new ways of thinking about life on earth. Now, as baby boomers face old age, a new door is being presented... the exploration of death and beyond. And with it, a new wave of teachers is boldly addressing this taboo topic.

If I had billions of dollars I would use it to launch death education programs that begin in pre-school and touch religious communities, social networks, political bodies and every aspect of life from childhood to old age. Medical schools would get special attention, so that we could teach doctors to stop seeing death as a failure.

In 2010, the wonderful PBS series *Frontline* aired a documentary called *Facing Death*, which followed several families facing life-or-death decisions for loved ones that had long since lost any quality of life. The program was well researched and well-produced, but it had one fatal flaw... not one of the doctors caring for these patients ever even mentioned hospice as an option. You can read the transcript of the entire film on line. A search for the word "hospice" only turns up one reference, when a doctor tells the family of a patient named John, "So things to think about would be, you know, to go home with a lot of support, with home hospice, would be a possibility, or not."[33]

Although the title of the film is *Facing Death*, there is an inside joke among many of my hospice colleagues when we talk about this film. We call it "Running Away from Death as Fast as Possible." PBS is very progressive and open-minded about controversial issues, and they have produced many brilliant documentaries that show death in a more positive light, including one of the most remarkable films I've ever seen, *The Suicide Tourist*.[34] There are several others, including *A Family Undertaking*[35] and *The Embrace of Dying*,[36] to name a few. It is a blessing that this information can be shared widely with the public, and slowly but surely, people are beginning to open up to the possibility that death is *not* the enemy. But that opening is not present anywhere in this film, and it gives a very clear picture of how resistant the medical establishment is to the idea of accepting death.

I have been blessed with the opportunity to do a lot of volunteer work in hospices and in hospitals, and along the way, I've had the chance to observe and compare the way death is addressed in both settings. With a few rare exceptions, the difference is night and day. I can't address this from a medical perspective because I'm not a nurse or a doctor, and I can't address it from a political perspective with any authority other than whatever authority I have as a private citizen. But I *can* address it from a spiritual and psychosocial perspective, and would like to offer my suggestions about how care can be better provided in this area.

First of all, contrary to popular misconception, hospice care is not just for people who are close to death, nor is it a place where someone "goes" to die (about 80% of hospice care takes place in the home).[37] Many hospices have transition programs for people with life-threatening illnesses who may have a year or more to live, and some in-patient hospice facilities care for patients who cannot get appropriate care in a hospital or nursing home for pain management or psychological issues. So it is important to understand that death is not necessarily imminent for hospice patients.

The first order of business would be to educate patients *and doctors* about what hospice is and is *not*. It is only in the last decade that medical schools have begun to include substantial training in end-of-life care as part of their curricula. If you ask most doctors over the age of 50 what they learned in medical school about helping people to die comfortably and consciously, they will shrug their shoulders and say, "Not a thing. It was never addressed. We are taught to avoid death."

Many people believe that the Hippocratic Oath[38] binds physicians to the idea of fending off death as a primary goal, but this is not actually true. There are two versions of the oath... the original one was written in the 6th century based on the teachings of Hippocrates, but there are several modern translations used today.

In the original, ancient version of the oath, physicians state the following:

"I will neither give a deadly drug to anybody who asked for it, nor will I make a suggestion to this effect. Similarly I will not give to a woman an abortive remedy."

71

This phrase does not appear in the modern translations, yet many doctors still believe that any action supporting or allowing death is a violation of their sacred oath. By contrast, today's oath has come a long way, and actually contains a line that prohibits physicians from pursuing pointless life-saving measures:[39]

"I will apply, for the benefit of the sick, all measures [that] are required, avoiding those twin traps of overtreatment and therapeutic nihilism."

It also says:

"Most especially must I tread with care in matters of life and death. If it is given me to save a life, all thanks. But it may also be within my power to take a life; this awesome responsibility must be faced with great humbleness and awareness of my own frailty."

Just as the Hippocratic Oath evolved over time, medical care in general is constantly changing as technology and social structures evolve. When my family doctor graduated from medical school in the 1970s, CT scans were just being invented. Also at that time, fewer than eight percent of physicians in the U.S. were women. But by 2011 women represented 47% of all first-year medical school students,[40] and the term "cat scan" had become a household word. Change does occur, but it occurs slowly, and it is now time to change the way we "do death."

Because medicine today is so compartmentalized, we are no longer under the care of a doctor, but a team of specialists that might include a cardiologist, anesthesiologist, internist and a nutritionist. These specialists pull out all the stops when it comes to keeping patients alive, and with today's technology, a body can be kept breathing on life support pretty much indefinitely, even if the consciousness has long since left the building.

Eventually, at some point, it may be decided that there's nothing more that can be done, and assuming the primary (attending) physician is enlightened enough to suggest hospice, at this point the medical team retreats and hands the patient over to hospice care.

Medical services (such as chemotherapy, surgery and other aggressive treatments) are replaced with hospice services (pain management and comfort measures only), so instead of life-saving interventions, the focus shifts to helping the patient face death as comfortably and as painlessly as possible. Many people refer to this stage as "palliative care," but that is a bit of a misnomer. Palliative medicine actually deals with pain management and alleviating suffering, regardless of whether or not the illness is life-threatening. A more accurate term to describe the care given at this stage would be "end-of-life" care or "transition management."

The team approach to health care can be compared to spokes on a wheel, and when a dying patient is "handed off" to the next specialist in line, that specialization – the next spoke – is usually hospice. But while hospice does an excellent job of managing the physical body and offers grief counseling for the bereaved, it does not always address the emotional, social and spiritual needs of the person who is dying. In this sense there is a spoke missing from the wheel... a specialist who acts as a "transition guide" to assist the person in crossing over. Hospice workers (nurses, doctors, social workers, chaplains and volunteers) are wonderfully compassionate and highly skilled, but they do not necessarily have the time or the training to perform the sacred task of guiding a dying patient across the threshold.

Whose Job is it Anyway?

I asked a recent medical school graduate – Dr. Jordan Justice, a second-year resident at the University of Arizona Medical Center – about the training he received in working with patients at the end of life. He told me that in his medical education, palliative care was an optional rotation (like an elective in college) for students planning to go into palliative medicine as a specialty, but was not required for all students. In his telling of it, end-of-life care was included in lectures related to pain management, pharmacology and psychiatry, but it was addressed primarily from the perspective of bio-ethics rather than emotional support or spiritual care. In Dr. Justice's words, "It's not really the doctor's role to transition the patients. I definitely see the need for a new job description that can be created for that role.

Just like the jobs of Physician's Assistant, Hospitalist and Nurse Practitioner are relatively new, there should be a new job description for helping patients face death."

In a September 2013 article in the *New York Times* opinion section,[41] writer David Bornstein points out the ways in which medical training is sorely lacking in compassion for both students and patients. Medical school and internships can be brutal for students, keeping them, as Bornstein describes, "sleep-deprived, overstressed, and in a state of fear of making mistakes, and sends the message that doubts or grief should be kept to oneself." He also describes the "socialization process" of doctors, which teaches them to be emotionally detached, aloof and even cynical, and suggests that the combination of hyper-competition and self-doubt in medical school can work against the development of compassionate and supportive relationships.

Bornstein tells the story of Dr. Rachel Naomi Remen,[42] who as a young intern broke down and cried while telling a couple that their three year-old child had died in the emergency room after a car accident. The hospital's chief resident was present during that conversation, and later took Remen aside to berate her for being "unprofessional" by showing so much emotion. Remen took the message to heart, and by the time she was a senior resident had turned that heart to stone when dealing with the emotions of patients and their loved ones.

But she did not want to continue her career in such an impervious state, nor did she want the expectation of imperviousness to be handed down to future medical students. So she developed a radical and unprecedented new curriculum called *The Healer's Art*, an elective medical school course that focuses on emotional sensitivity and grief awareness. When she first started the course, which began as a small, informal group of community physicians, she was afraid the university dean would find out and throw her out. But she wasn't thrown out, and instead, the course expanded, and is now taught at half of America's medical schools. Of the 13,000 students who've gone through the course, the majority say that it bridged a gap in their medical education.

These students are being trained to work with grief... their own as well as the grief of those they serve. But until our hospitals fill up with a new generation of doctors who've had this type of training, we're still missing an important spoke in the wheel.... *a transition team.*

When a patient is actively dying and family members are present, it is extremely helpful when a skilled, compassionate person can be at the bedside coaching, comforting and supporting everybody involved, but as Dr. Justice pointed out, this is not a physician's role. Hospice nurses can sometimes provide this service, but at an in-patient facility they are far too busy, and home visits from nurses are for taking care of the patient's physical rather than emotional needs. The missing spoke of the wheel is a transition guide or death midwife who can not only help the family understand the processes that occur as death advances, but can help the patient navigate the various levels of consciousness that he or she may be experiencing. Some patients or families may request the help of their personal priest or pastor, who can offer prayers and perhaps theological teachings, but most members of the clergy are not trained in death midwifery or clinical chaplaincy.

Enter the hospice or hospital chaplain. The chaplain has specific training in compassionate listening and the art of spiritual conversation, and is well-qualified to be part of a transition team. But chaplaincy brings with it a whole new set of challenges, because a patient's spiritual outlook is often very difficult to determine based on what box they check under "religion" on the hospital intake form. According to the 2008 *Pew Research: Religion and Public Life Project:* [43]

- More than 1/4 of American adults (28%) have left the faith in which they were raised in favor of another religion - or no religion at all.

- If change in affiliation from one type of Protestantism to another is included, 44% of adults have either switched religious affiliation, moved from being unaffiliated with any religion to being affiliated with a particular faith, or dropped any connection to a specific religious tradition altogether.

- One-in-four Americans between the ages of 18-29 say they are not currently affiliated with any particular religion.

During my training as a hospital chaplain, I observed that the majority of patients listed their religion as "none" (granted, this was in Oregon, a notoriously progressive state. The statistics would probably be different in Mississippi or Oklahoma). Even though they were "nones," when I visited them and a conversation ensued, it turned out that they had spiritual beliefs and practices, such as the belief in an afterlife, a meditation practice or an affinity with New Thought, Wicca or some other system that defies categorization. Several told me they'd had near-death experiences or had received communication from a departed loved one, and that prayer to a divine source was very important to them.

Hospital intake forms (and the computer databases to which they're connected) are extremely limited in this area. Some offer multiple choice selections that include only mainstream religious groups, and the system won't allow variations such as "atheist" or "pagan." Others allow patients to write-in their choices, but because some spiritual belief systems (including my own) cannot be put neatly into a doctrinal box, the only option may be to select "none" or "other." This does not give a chaplain much to go on when trying to get a sense of what might be spiritually comforting to a patient. My personal preference whenever I'm asked to choose a religion is to answer, "all of them," following the lead of folk music legend Woody Guthrie, who spent a good portion of his later life in hospitals. When he was asked to claim a religious affiliation, he'd say "all," and as the story goes, at least one hospital refused to admit him until he selected an approved religion (I met his granddaughter Sarah in 2012 and she verified this story. It is part of the Guthrie family legacy).

Changes to Chaplaincy

When I visit a patient and introduce myself as one of the hospital chaplains, mainstream Protestants are usually delighted to have a chaplain visit (Catholics are treated as a separate entity and only visited by Catholic chaplains or priests, which is a whole other story). But when I visit the "nones," the "others" or a Jewish patient, these are their typical responses:

"I don't need a chaplain. I'm Jewish."
"I'm not religious."
"I don't believe in God."
"No thanks."

Because it is my job to open a dialog with patients in which they can feel safe sharing their feelings (religion often turns out to be irrelevant), I reply to these responses with casualness and humor to break the ice. If they say, "I'm not religious," I reply with, "Neither am I." When they say, "I don't believe in God," I say, "I understand. I don't believe in *that* God either." When they say they're Jewish, they are surprised when I tell them that there are Jewish chaplains.

This addresses something that is calling out for change in the field of clinical chaplaincy. Most non-Christians, when asked if they'd like to see a chaplain, will say no because they think someone will walk in with a Bible and a cross hoping to save a soul. This impression comes from the misconception that the term "chaplain" refers only to Christian clergy. But in reality, chaplains come in all spiritual flavors and do not preach or pray for salvation (unless a patient specifically requests it). On a typical shift at the hospital, I might discuss reincarnation with a Buddhist, pray for healing with an evangelical Christian, lead a Jewish person in a guided meditation to help him relax, or chat with an atheist about his medical condition or family concerns. A clinical chaplain's job is to support whatever belief system the patient embraces, and our intention is always to meet patients *where they are.*

It is my experience that the word "chaplain" throws many people off and deprives them of an opportunity to share their feelings with a trained listener. My solution is to find another term that does not carry so much religious baggage. My preference is to use the term "spiritual counselor," and although I have not seen a formal study of this, I would bet that the *nones* and the *others* would respond far more favorably to a visit by a spiritual counselor than a chaplain. But even the word "spiritual" is loaded for a lot of people, so just as "chaplain" might scare off a Jew or a spiritualist, the term "spiritual" can be just as off-putting for a mainstream Christian or an atheist.

Perhaps the solution is to come up with a purely secular term that would neutralize the whole thing. If I introduced myself to patients as "part of the hospital's emotional support team," all the charge would be removed, and then, during the course of the conversation, the question of spirituality could be introduced. As chaplains, we are trained to ask, after an appropriate amount of small talk, "Is there any spiritual or religious practice that is meaningful to you?" And from there we follow the patient's lead.

Countless studies have shown that finding some sort of spiritual meaning, or at the very least, having a chance to engage in a dialog about feelings, beliefs and/or questions related to the meaning of one's life, is enormously comforting for the sick and dying.[44,45] But sometimes, particularly in hospice care, the patients are non-verbal, non-responsive, or essentially unconscious (though they can still hear and feel the presence of those around them). There is still a lot we can do to comfort these folks, such as praying either out loud or silently, bringing in some soothing music, reading from poetry or sacred texts, or singing their favorite hymns, chants or songs.

But if all we have in the chart is "none" as a description of their spiritual views, and there are no family members present to tell us about the patient's spiritual preferences, we are at a huge disadvantage. I have no way of knowing whether a non-responsive patient would prefer harp music, a Shamanic ceremony, a Buddhist chant or a reading from Psalms. We also don't often know much about a patient's other preferences, for example, would they want the TV on in their room, or not? Some people keep the television on constantly as background noise in their homes, so for them, the sound of TV might be comforting. For me, it would be the most annoying sound on earth. If I was unconscious in a bed somewhere, the last thing I'd want in my ears is the sound of television commercials. It would be just as disruptive to my consciousness as reading to me about God's wrath in Deuteronomy or some other religious tome that doesn't align with my spiritual outlook. And in clinical chaplaincy, our work is all always about honoring the patient's own consciousness, and never about imposing our own preferences.

My friend Gene is a hospice chaplain in the deep South. A brilliant, educated and enlightened man, he recently told me a story that illustrates this point perfectly. A 51 year-old woman – I'll call her Lynn – was admitted to his in-patient hospice facility, dying from cancer. Gene spent weeks getting to know Lynn, and she revealed that the evangelical Christian upbringing of her childhood had been full of superstition and terror for her, and included physical abuse by the church leaders. She now rejected religion completely, but Gene, through many hours of pastoral conversation and counseling, was able to help Lynn find a spiritual sense of the divine *within herself* that was peaceful and comforting, without any mention of God, Jesus, scripture or anything related to the negative experiences of her childhood.

One day Gene came to make his rounds at the hospice (Lynn was in and out of consciousness and close to death by this point), and noticed that all the televisions in all the rooms had been turned on and tuned in to *The 700 Club*, including the television in Lynn's room! Gene flew into a rage, yelling at the staff and demanding to find out who did this. It turned out that one of the new volunteers had quietly gone from room to room turning on the program in the hope of saving the souls of the patients before they died.

The volunteer, of course, was promptly fired. But the damage to Lynn could not be undone. Actively dying people can hear everything around them, and in Lynn's vulnerable and open state of mind as she was moving between dimensions, Gene knew that the words she heard from the TV would have triggered her old fears. He spent the next few days by her side, speaking soothing words and helping to guide her soul through a peaceful transition.

The solution (aside from better screening and training for volunteers) is to provide a detailed intake questionnaire about what brings a patient comfort (songs, poems, readings, religious practices, etc). Gene and I came up with the following questions that could be asked of patients who are seriously ill or dying in the event that they become unable to make their emotional, environmental, psychosocial and spiritual needs known:

Environmental

- What kind of temperatures are comfortable for you? Do you prefer light or heavy blankets? Window open or closed?

- How do you feel about having the TV on in your room? If you enjoy having it on, what kind of programming do you prefer or not prefer?

- Would you enjoy music playing in your room? If so, what type of music, and what pieces, songs or artists would you want to listen to?

Spiritual

- What, if any, religious or spiritual traditions or affiliations do you align with? Please be as specific as possible.

- Would you enjoy hearing music from that tradition played for you?

- Please list or describe any readings that are spiritually or emotionally comforting for you.

- Would you enjoy a visit with a spiritual care provider (counselor, teacher, healer or minister) from your preferred tradition? Please tell us what sort of provider this might be.

- Would you welcome a guided meditation to help you relax and to guide you through your transition?

PsychoSocial

- Is it important that someone is at your bedside all or most of time, or would you prefer to spend more time alone?

- Are you comfortable with multiple visitors in your room, or would you prefer only one or two at a time?

- If you are dying, who – if anybody – would you like to have at your bedside? You may also wish to be alone during this sacred transition. If that is your preference, please let us know.

Emotional

- Have you discussed your death with your loved ones? If not, would you like a transition counselor to assist you in having this conversation?

- Are there any loved ones in your life with whom you feel you need to make peace? If so, would you like a transition counselor to assist you with this?

- Have you told your loved ones of your preferences in terms of burial, cremation, memorial service and other plans related to your death?
- If there is anything in particular you'd like your loved ones to do in terms of honoring their grief in response to your passing?

- These are just a few suggestions, but as you can see, having the answers to these questions can make a big difference in the bedside experience, and can assist with the grieving process for those left behind, knowing that they honored their loved ones wishes at the end of life.

NOTES

[23]http://www.deathisnottheenemy.com/Portals/1777/CS%20Resources/CS%20Native%20American%20Dying%20and%20Death.pdf
[24] Johnson, Judith. "The Secret Component of Grief." TheHuffingtonPost.com. 25 Oct. 2012.
[25] http://drparisetti.com/
[26] http://psychcentral.com/blog/archives/2013/05/31/how-the-dsm-5-got-grief-bereavement-right/
[27] *What has Become of Grief Counseling? An Evaluation of the Empirical Foundations of the New Pessimism.* Professional Psychology: Research and Practice, 38, 347–355

[28] Currier, Joseph M., Robert A. Neimeyer, and Jeffrey S. Berman. "The Effectiveness of Psychotherapeutic Interventions for Bereaved Persons: A Comprehensive Quantitative Review." *Psychological Bulletin* 134.5 (2008)

[29] www.drgaryschwartz.com/files/QuickSiteImages/BeischelEXPLORE2007vol3.pdf

[30] Leviticus 19:31 ESV

[31] Leviticus 20:27 ESV

[32] Deuteronomy 18:14 ESV

[33] www.pbs.org/wgbh/pages/frontline/facing-death/etc/transcript.html. It is also noted in the transcript that this patient *did* choose hospice as an option. In the words of the narrator, "John… did agree to go to hospice. One day later, he would die." The choice of words, the tone of voice and the overall feeling of how this was presented, in my opinion, suggested that going to hospice is a form of "giving up" and/or hastening death.

[34] http://www.pbs.org/wgbh/pages/frontline/suicidetourist/

[35] http://www.pbs.org/pov/afamilyundertaking/

[36] http://embraceofaging.com/Dying/embrace_dying.html

[37] Hospice Myths & Facts | Florida Hospice & Palliative Care Association. *Florida Hospice Palliative Care Association Hospice Myths Facts Comments.*

[38] http://www.pbs.org/wgbh/nova/body/hippocratic-oath-today.html

[39] Written in 1964 by Louis Lasagna, Academic Dean of the School of Medicine at Tufts University (used in many medical schools today).

[40] http://www.catalyst.org/knowledge/women-medicine

[41] Bornstein, David. "Medicine's Search for Meaning." *Opinionator Medicines Search for Meaning Comments*. New York Times, 18 Sept. 2013.Web.19 Dec. 2013. http://opinionator.blogs.nytimes.com/2013/09/18/medicines-search-for-meaning/?_r=0

[42] Remen is a clinical professor of family and community medicine at the U.C.S.F. School of Medicine and the director of the Institute for the Study of Health and Wellness.

[43] Summary of Key Findings. *Statistics on Religion in America Report*. Pew Research: Religion and Public Life Project. 2008. http://religions.pewforum.org/reports

[44] http://www.nytimes.com/2008/10/29/nyregion/29hospice.html?pagewanted=all

[45] http://www.ncbi.nlm.nih.gov/pmc/articles/PMC1466687/

6. Adjusting Our Line of Sight

"Previous cultures understood the transformative nature of pain. In our society, pain has become an aspect of the shadow, to be escaped at all costs. We are increasingly conditioned to seek someone to blame for our suffering, which in the United States has become linked with material greed as an incentive to sue someone for one's suffering. To blame someone else is not to honor one's own experience. To deny the value of suffering is to close the door on transformation that can only come through pain.

"Moving beyond instinctual and cultural conditioning to avoid pain, we honor the transpersonal dimension of our Self, which is beyond the dualities of pleasure and pain. We welcome the reality of love, which embraces every aspect of life with the wholeness of the Self. In allowing the pain of longing, we allow our Self to be taken into the innermost chamber of the heart... Some people who like to live in their own darkness can become addicted to suffering, just as they can become addicted to their psychological problems. Pain like this, to which one becomes attached, is not transformative pain"

From *Sufism: The Transformation of the Heart*
by *Llewellyn Vaughan-Lee*[46]

"Your safety – nobody's safety – comes from anything on earth. The more you realize that you are here to find your way back home, the more the true source of safety can be understood."

A channeled message from Danny

Turning the corner on Grief Street is all about a shift in perspective, and sometimes a shift in perspective can be as simple as finding new language to express our feelings and ideas. Many of the bereaved who are addicted to their pain will say things like, "It will never be OK," or "I will never get over it." I spoke to a woman just yesterday who said, "I cannot rejoice when someone dies."

This might be an appropriate comment if we'd been talking about the death of a child or someone who died unexpectedly and tragically. But we were talking about the death of Sylvia Browne, a world-famous psychic medium who taught millions about the beauty of the afterlife. Sylvia died in November 2013, and a group us were talking about how all the happy wishes and blessings we were sending to her on her journey. If anybody would be joyous about going to the Other Side, it would be Sylvia Browne. Yet the woman I was speaking with saw the death as "sad sad news." I suspect she didn't even know who Sylvia was, but either way, her reaction seemed like a knee-jerk response based on her social programming that death is *always* sad.

Nelson Mandela died a few weeks after Sylvia Browne did, and comments were broadcast all over social media from all over the world. Most of them talked about feeling sad. My response to this was, "Why are you sad?"

I feel nothing but joy when I think of Nelson Mandela. He died at age 95 and left behind a brilliant legacy. Did people expect him to live forever? This man had a beautiful, timely death and a long, meaningful life. I challenge anybody to show me one good reason to be sad. I have asked several people to explain their sadness, and their responses range from "it shows respect" to "it's sad that he will no longer be in the world." Interestingly, none of those people believe that a soul or some sort of consciousness lives on after physical death.

I find these responses to be mindless and robotic. Mandela did more for the world than most people could ever imagine doing. He did what he came here to do, and physical world no longer requires his presence. His life and death do not ask for our sadness as a sign of respect. They require only our joy and gratitude. Sadness showing respect makes no sense at all. The dead do not want us to be sad! The most respect we can show them is to support their continued journey with as much love and reverence as possible. I certainly understand the sadness experienced by those who must learn to live without the physical manifestation of a beloved companion or family member. But I don't understand why we suffer over the natural death, via aging and illness, of celebrities and political figures with whom we had no personal relationship and whose contribution to humanity is now complete. I felt the same way when Pope John Paul II died in 2005 and millions of people worldwide were devastated by his death at age 84.

Social scientist Peter Marris in his book *Loss and Change*, says, "The impulse to defend the predictability of life is a fundamental and universal principle of human psychology."[47] While this impulse may be fundamental and perhaps absolute, I think it is the responsibility of grief counselors and spiritual care providers to assist clients in learning how to release attachment to this impulse in order to move forward in the healing process when loss or trauma occurs.

Marris also says:

> When a pattern of relationships is disrupted in any way for which we are not fully prepared, the thread of continuity in the loss may fundamentally threaten the integrity of the structure of meanings on which this continuity rests, and cannot be acknowledged without distress. But if life is to go on, the continuity must somehow be restored. When loss is irretrievable, there must be a reinterpretation of what we have learned about our purposes and attachments—and the principles which underlie the regularity of experience—radical enough to trace out the thread again.
>
> To do this, the loss must first be accepted as something we have to understand—not just as an event that has happened, but also as a series of events that we must now *expect* to happen, and a retrospect of earlier events whose familiar meaning has not been shadowed by our changed circumstances. The conservative impulse will make us seek to deny the loss. But that impulse fails, it will also lead us to repair the thread, tying the past, present and future together again with rewoven strands of meaning.

Turning the corner on Grief Street is all about a radical reinterpretation of our beliefs, and such a shift can easily begin with a simple change in language. A competent counselor might suggest looking for a few new phrases, such as "I will never be the same," and "I will never find it acceptable that my child died in this way." We can accept that it is unacceptable. We can accept that we will be changed. And from that place, we can continue to *live,* and even find joy again.

The Voices of Change

As a result of the Facebook debacle of 2011, I was prompted to make two significant decisions:

1. Write a book called *Turning the Corner on Grief Street.*
2. Post and enforce "house rules" in the Facebook group to help ensure that the people who wish to join the group are fully aware of our point of view.

The group has since tripled in size, and the overall attitude of the members is open-hearted, intelligent and deeply mystical. I thought it would be fitting to open this chapter with some current comments that express a completely different mindset than what we saw in the comments in Chapter 3.

These are reproduced exactly as written. I haven't changed the wording, spelling or punctuation, though the comments have been edited for brevity (and the names have been changed):

Veronica

I have lost both of my kids. The first was 9 years ago to suicide. That experience prompted me to seek more spiritual knowledge... there was no way I was going to believe he was just "gone forever." Three years ago I lost my daughter to cancer. Through caring for her during her illness I learned a lot about forgiveness and love and courage and a host of other things. I truly feel blessed to have been "chosen" by them." I am grateful for all of it. People think I am some kind of "hero," but I am not. They can't understand why I am not just a lump of depressed flesh. I have to say it's because of my spiritual beliefs, and most assuredly because I STILL have a relationship with my kids.

Beverly

I believe I was being prepped to go through this. I lost my daughter 18 months ago at 34. About 7 years ago, I started on a spiritual journey when I had a glimpse of what the other side is like. It is still hard, but I know that if she feels half as good as I felt then, I have no doubt that she is just fine.

Diane

People seek me out when they are lost in grief and it makes my heart swell when they describe receiving messages from their loved ones. The light comes on in their eyes when they understand that they just experienced a "hello from heaven." I would not be in a position to help if I had not gone through these things. This is not to say that I do not go through the same grief process as anyone else...I do. It's just that I know the purpose of it, I am able to just ride out the storm. I do not run from it.

Sarah

It is amazing to see how many of you are like me! I am not able to participate in those grief groups anymore because my experience is so different from theirs. My son "died" in March 2004. Had it not been for him, I would not have found my gifts and would not be helping others connect with their loved ones.

Judy

I truly believe death is to help many get on their path. It helps us to become in touch with our own inner light. I understand how hard it is, but it is an avenue to help us find who we are etc.

Marcia

My relationship with my son did not *end* when he died... it just kept existing across dimensions, and there is actually MORE love, because the love is not weighed down with the heaviness of the 3-D universe... expectations, projections, fears and all the stuff that clutters up relationships on earth. I'm so glad to have so many of like mind here. A conversation like this in most grief groups would cause a riot!

Jonathan

Marcia, you are right about the grief groups. It is so frustrating to see people stuck for years in the same place. I have quit many of those groups for that very reason. People who could otherwise be helped turn out to be "causalities" of these groups.

Annie

I think the stages of grief as described by Elizabeth Kubler Ross, when not properly understood, can turn grief into a competitive sport, even to the point where I feared that progress would be misconstrued as if I didn't love my departed as much as others.

Shireen

I believe my son's death was a spiritual lesson for me. I began studying about the afterlife with a passion. I get signs from him all the time. Now I reach out to other parents who lost a child. I explain what I learned about the signs. This is now my life's purpose. I couldn't have been prepared had I not suffered the loss of a child myself.

Karyn

Without a doubt, my daughter's death was part of a bigger plan for my spiritual evolution. One of the first messages I got from her was that there were things she needed to do on the other side and things I needed to do here that I could not do until she had crossed over. She instructed me to complete projects that were undone and to write books to help others. I moved quickly into "acceptance" because I was having the experience of her spirit touch my life. It is not saying "I like this better," or "I'm glad this happened," It is simply saying "It IS."

Ron

Karyn, I have seen bereaved mothers who will be probably hang onto their grief the rest of their lives. It's like they wear their misery as a badge of honor, as if they are demonstrating their love for the child by being as miserable as possible for as long as possible. I have not lost a child, so I don't know EXACTLY what they are going through, but as a grief counselor, I can see they are stuck when they construct a wall of hostility around them. There is so much help available, even just a reading with a medium.

Veronica

Ron, I have noticed the same thing with some grieving parents... they wear their grief as a badge of honor, and that also applies to other areas of life where they are "stuck." I know people who suffer from various physical ailments who wear their pain like a badge of honor, or their food allergies, or all kinds of other things. Some people can find peace with anything that happens, while others just get grumpier and grumpier. Maybe that is the life they chose to lead in this incarnation... Maybe they incarnated to experience a life of hopelessness and pain, which would bring forth a particular set of lessons.

Ron

That is certainly a common lesson we learn through incarnation Veronica, and we all work with that lesson in different forms. The "badge of honor" thing is a form of addiction. One can be addicted to pain and suffering as easily as one can be addicted to alcohol or drugs. It's all a way of avoiding being fully conscious.

At a dinner party recently I sat next to a man whose young son had died a few years earlier. He told me a story that exemplifies what being "fully conscious" might look like in the face of death and grief. He described himself as a person with a scientific mind, and although he accepted the idea of a soul that continues to exist after bodily death, he still grappled with a need to find empirical explanations of what a soul is, what frequency it resonates on and how it is able to communicate with us. But he also struggled with the down-to-earth questions, primarily about how, as an American male, he should behave in the face of grief. After spending some time working with a grief counselor, he had this wonderful revelation:

"I always believed I had to be a rock for my family, eternally strong and unbreakable. But one day I realized that holding on to this view of myself was actually hindering the healing for my wife and extended family members. I realized we were all part of a huge, flowing river, and my loved ones were like the rocks and boulders in the river, allowing the water to flow over them. But I saw myself as the biggest, tallest rock, planted squarely in the middle of the river, forcing the water to divert *around* me. Instead of going with the flow, I was actually obstructing the flow, trying to make it bend to my will."

This man had come to see himself – and his reaction to grief – in a new way. His experience exemplifies the tasks of grieving as described by Worden 1981 and Parks & Weiss 1983.[48] The first three involve accepting the loss (overcoming denial), working through the pain of grief (doing grief work), and intellectual acceptance (understanding what has happened). The next two tasks include a change in identity and a shift in the degree of emotional attachment. For the man described above, the shift in identity, in his *perception*, transformed him from an immovable boulder to a stone in a flowing river.

Danny's Bed

In some of the 2011 Facebook comments from angry grievers, I was accused of being a bad mother, emotionally detached, not in touch with my feelings and not grieving properly because I don't identify as a "bereaved parent." In some of my responses to these charges, I attempted to educate my critics on the difference between *detachment* and *non-attachment.* Those of you who've read my previous books are familiar with my personal grief journey and know that I don't have a heart of stone, so there's no need to revisit that here. But this is a good place to explore how it's possible to experience a traumatic loss and emerge whole and healthy rather than bitter and broken.

Let's start by examining the difference between *non-attachment* and *detachment:*

Detachment
Indifferent, apathetic and/or uninterested. A person who is truly detached has no interest in the subject matter or the outcome of the situation, and there is no emotional involvement of any kind. As an example, I am totally detached when it comes to football. I don't know (or care) who the teams are or who wins a game. I've never even watched a football game. I am utterly detached from football.

Non-attachment:
Connection, acknowledgement and honoring of the issue, and able to accept the outcome without clinging to the desired outcome. Using the football example, if I was a fan, I would enjoy watching a game for entertainment, and although I'd be disappointed if my team lost, I would accept it. I might mourn the loss of the money I bet on the game, but I would find a way to incorporate that loss into my world and work with it.

In terms of bereavement, it is hard to imagine that anybody could experience true *detachment* concerning the death of a loved one. In that case, the detachment would probably be a defense mechanism to block off strong painful feelings. Some of my detractors have accused me of this, because as Veronica so eloquently stated above, "They can't understand why I am not just a lump of depressed flesh."

The people quoted in the above comments express what I consider to be a healthy form of non-attachment. They are in touch with their pain, they feel their feelings, and they honor those feelings by allowing them in, sitting with them for a period of time, then letting them go with love and reverence. They know the waves of sadness will visit again, and that the cycle of allowing, accepting and releasing will continue forever, and they accept it.

My friend Mike gives an excellent example of how misunderstood healthy non-attachment can be. Someone told him that he was being "callous" because he seemed so unattached to the trauma surrounding the suicide attempts of both of his sons in the same year. His answer was:

"I became less attached when I started to notice what thoughts were bringing me sadness. Once I saw that they were nothing but guilt thoughts of "should" and "shouldn't," those thoughts just left me. It doesn't mean we don't do everything we can to help another, but we get to a point where we can't join in their suffering anymore. That is when we can be of the most help and simply be there in pure presence and unconditional love for them... without judging them or ourselves."

A few weeks after he said this, Mike's dog died, and although he was devastated to lose his beloved companion of 14 years, he found himself deeply pondering the nature of his grief. He began to examine his sad thoughts and discovered that they were always about *his* needs, or in his words, "completely selfish." He realized that his grief was all about *him,* and when he realized this, he had to laugh at the lack of respect it showed for the soul of the dog and *its* needs. When our own needs are stripped away momentarily, we are left with nothing but gratitude for the blessings that soul shared with us. Mike was able to see this and shift his attachment to non-attachment. But most of us are so afraid of being perceived as callous or heartless that we aren't willing to take that step. The good news is that there are tasks, tools and techniques for working through grief that do not render us heartless, but actually open our hearts to more love and deeper understanding of the "lost" relationship.

Clinical psychologist and thanatologist Therese A. Rando[49] identifies the following six primary tasks of grieving. It is important to remember that these tasks are not necessarily experienced in order, and that any individual may have difficulty or get "stuck" anywhere on the spectrum:

1. Recognize the loss
For someone dealing with a life-threatening diagnosis, recognizing the loss may come in the form of accepting the prognosis and researching the illness and treatment options in order to become educated about what to expect as the illness progresses. For a sudden death, recognizing the loss may come in the form of identifying the body, or viewing the body as part of a memorial service. This is part of the reason we have rituals... to gather the community together in recognition of the transition that has occurred. The woman I mentioned in Chapter Five who refused to look at her son's body or attend his funeral is a good example of how some people are not willing to recognize the loss.

2. React to the separation
What I love about the story of the Native Americans in the ICU in Chapter 5 is that they reacted to the separation in a natural, uncensored way. Feeling and expressing our grief is vitally important to the process of healing. Non-attachment does not mean non-reactive.

3. Recollect and re-experience the deceased and the relationship
It is a popular practice these days for a friend or family member to prepare a slide show of photos from a person's life to show at a memorial service. This is a wonderful way for the community to recollect and re-experience together. This can also be done with people who are terminally ill by looking at old family photos with them, talking about their lives, and perhaps even keeping a written or digitally recorded journal of their recollections to share with future generations.

4. Relinquish the old attachments to the deceased and the old world

We have all heard about (or experienced) the difficulty of facing a dead child's empty room or a dead spouse's empty office. This is particularly difficult when it comes time to alter that room or office in some way, such as getting rid of the person's clothes or belongings, or re-purposing the room for a new use. This is when ritual becomes a valuable tool. One way to relinquish old attachments while still keeping our loved one's spirit close to us is to create a ritual around the shifting of items that are attached to the deceased and our previous life. See Chapter Nine for specific details on rituals that are very effective for this process.

5. Readjust to the new world without forgetting the old

Many bereaved people are told that they must "move on," "get over it" or "let go" in order to continue their lives, and it is a shame that these terms are used so carelessly. Moving on and letting go does not mean that we leave our deceased loved ones behind. It means that we integrate their presence into our reality in a new way. After the death of a close friend or loved one, we are forced to occupy a new world in which they are physically absent. But as many discover, that new world can be filled with emotional and spiritual riches that would have been previously unavailable. The spirits of our loved ones are present in that new world with us.

6. Reinvest

What does reinvesting look like? If we use a financial model for the concept of *investing,* it looks like placing our energy and assets into something new and possibly risky in the hope that it will pay off in some way. The assets we risk in the grief process are our belief systems about how the world works. If we're willing to risk those, the payoff is enormous.

Using my own grief experience as an example of how these tasks might express themselves, my reactions to my son's illness and death followed Rando's steps, but not necessarily in order. Because I was dealing with anticipatory grief, many of these steps took place while he was still alive. With his diagnosis I *recognized* the loss. In preparing for the years ahead, I *reacted* to our pending separation, and the inevitability to his death. During the his illness and physical degeneration, we, together, *recollected* and *re-experienced* our relationship by creating photo albums and a memory quilt, talking and meditating together, visiting old friends and acquiring memorable experiences. Also during this time, I *relinquished attachments* to our old world through a variety of rituals that helped me release those attachments (see Chapter Nine). After his death I *recollected* and *re-experienced* our relationship again, trying to adapt to its new form, ultimately *reinvesting* in myself by going back to school to study theology and become a hospice chaplain.

On the other end of the spectrum are those who have not learned, through self-study, spiritual guidance or appropriate counseling, to practice non-attachment. As an example, if you've ever attended a conference for the national bereavement group *The Compassionate Friends*, you'll know that many of the attendees use the phrase "Joey's dad" or "Bereaved Mom" as the title printed on their name badges. For this type of conference, especially for the newly bereaved, this is a beautiful idea and can be a healthy way of acknowledging the grief event. However, I have seen this concept taken to extremes when people attach to the role of bereaved parent as their primary identity. I know one woman who lost an infant 27 years ago, and still attends these conferences every year wearing the baby's picture and the name "Melissa's mom" on her badge in lieu of her own name. While this may be one way to honor the deceased, it also makes the statement that the bereaved person has not found a new identity. Many people have a belief operating just below their conscious awareness that identifying as yourself in your new life somehow dishonors the deceased, when in fact, just the opposite is true. I can't say this enough... *our departed loved ones want us to become new people and live complete, fulfilling lives.*

I now want to share a brief story of what I think non-attachment can look like in bereavement, at least the way it looks for *me*, in my own life.

My son Danny died at age 16 in 2006 after being seriously ill and severely disabled for nearly half of his life. I have moved across the country and lived in a few different places since then, because my life changed radically after his death, ultimately leading me to a new path as an author, spiritual teacher, minister and hospice worker. Last year I moved again, downsizing from a three-bedroom house to a one-bedroom apartment. I sold or gave away most of my furniture and possessions, including Danny's bed.

I had no idea how strong the feelings would be about letting go of that bed. The day I put the ad on Craigslist to sell it, I wrapped myself in one of Danny's old blankets, lay down on the bed, and immediately started sobbing, feeling a mixture of guilt (for letting the bed go), sadness, loneliness and grief. I could feel Danny there with me, and could feel all the energy of our deep love held in the fibers of that bed. I missed him so much it was unbearable. I had slept in that bed with him for hundreds of nights while he suffered through his illness. He died in that bed, and afterward, I continued to sleep there, dreaming, channeling, meditating and receiving the first messages he sent me from the Other Side. Letting go of that bed ripped my heart out, because it felt as if being without it would somehow separate me from him.

It was deep, deep pain, but it was *good* pain, and it was exactly what I needed. It had been a long time since I had touched into that degree of despair, and as I teach others, pain opens our hearts and can actually heal us if we recognize its deeper purpose. Like most people, I go through my busy life in a sort of numb state most of the time, taking care of earthly business and functioning more or less reasonably in the world. But every once in a while I catch a glimpse of that grief, like I did that day with Danny's bed, and it is like a welcome visit from a dear old friend. I say to my grief, "Oh there you are. I haven't seen much of you lately. Welcome into my heart. I accept you and honor you. Stay and visit for a while." It hurts, but it is alive, vibrant and healthy. I'm not afraid of it. It keeps me open and human. It is a state of grace.

But I can also let go of it. I can hold my grief in a place of honor in my heart with an open invitation for it to grab hold of me whenever necessary. But the grief is not my *identity*. I am not a "bereaved person." I am a mother who experienced the death of a child.

That is non-attachment.

Changing the Way We Look at the Afterlife

In 2010 I created a non-profit organization called The Afterlife Education Foundation. Each year we produce an annual conference[50] that features leading spiritual teachers, psychic mediums, religious scholars and scientific researchers who are involved in studying the survival of consciousness after death. One of my favorite presentations at the conference is called *Heaven: A History,* in which grief counselors and religious scholars examine the imagery and beliefs that most people hold about an afterlife. It explores notions of heaven vs. hell, judgment, eternal reward vs. eternal punishment, sin vs. salvation, and other mainstream Judeo-Christian concepts.

In this section I would like to dispel a few of the key myths and superstitions that can stand it the way of healthy grieving for some people. Let's start with angels.

Angels

Among other questions, *Heaven: A History* explores the origin of the idea that people turn into angels when they die. Where did this idea come from? It is not rooted in the Bible or church doctrine, nor is it present in most other religions or cultures. Yet it is embraced passionately by many bereaved individuals, especially when the person who died was a child.

The idea to address this topic at the conference was inspired by the many conversations I've either observed or facilitated in which people refer to their deceased loved ones as having "received their angel wings" when they died. Some people even refer to the anniversary date of the death as an "angelversary," to mark the day the person became an angel.

Researching the origin of this idea is fascinating, since it does not appear in Western religious teachings (or Eastern, to the best of my knowledge). Mormonism is a possible exception, which, as I understand it, believes that the angel Moroni was once a human being, Adam is now the archangel Michael, and Noah is now the archangel Gabriel.[51] But even if this belief is pervasive, it seems to apply only to significant religious figures, and not to average folks.

Most religions acknowledge that there are angels in the higher realms, but they are not the souls of dead humans. They are a completely unique and different energetic form, and people do not turn into angels when they die. So where does this imagery come from, and what value does it provide for grievers?

My best guess is that somewhere along the way in the development of theology, the idea of a soul or spirit got mixed up with the idea of an angel, and now millions of people have conflated them into the same thing. Seeing your beloved departed as an angel offers comfort because it assigns the dead person an elevated status of being good, kind and loving... like an angel. Personally, I think it can be detrimental to the grieving process because it does not help us understand death in a realistic or healthy way. Imagining our dead loved ones with wings and halos may be comforting, but it can also be a feeble form of comfort at best, in much the same way a friend or family member might say, "Your child died because God needed another angel in heaven." I remember a movie in which Nicole Kidman played a mother whose young child died. She attended a grief recovery group in which someone offered that silly platitude, and she replied, "If God needed another angel, he could have just *made* one."

Here's another theory... I think it might have originated with the plagues in Europe. That's where a lot of western culture's fear of death originated, because the deaths were so gruesome and horrifying. I'm wondering if the angel idea emerged as a way to make people feel better about witnessing so many ghastly deaths. Rather than a decaying, pain-filled body, the bereaved could imagine their dead loved ones in a much more beautiful form as a sparkling clean, radiant angel. It definitely would have provided comfort to people at the time.

Then again, the whole idea might have come from the 1946 movie *It's a Wonderful Life,* in which model citizen George Bailey works with a guardian angel whose mission is to help George "earn his wings." Hollywood has a lot of influence on our religious imagery. If you doubt that, just conjure up an image of Moses for one second. I bet he looks a lot like Charlton Heston in the 1956 movie, *The Ten Commandments.*

So what are angels, really?

Angels are beings of light, and they have a different purpose. If you study religious texts you will see that they act as messengers, healers and intercessors. In a channeled message I received from Danny, I was told that angels are like transmitters that move energy around, sending and receiving light. They are resonators for light and their job is to keep the frequencies clear. They are keepers of light.

I asked Steffany Barton, a registered nurse who is also a medium and angel communicator,[52] to share her thoughts about angels, and this is what she said:

Mention the word "angel," and a myriad of images rush to mind. From halos and wings to robes and harps, the notion of these perfect, pure heavenly hosts has captivated the human imagination for centuries. Angels seem to form a perfect bridge between mundane and Divine. So who are these beings? What makes an angel?

The word "angel" in Hebrew is *mal'ak,* which means *messenger.* In the spiritual and religious context, this messenger brings news from God, Source, the One. Angels are beings of pure energy who bear light and bring forth peace, comfort, and rest. Non-physical by nature but able to appear seemingly in the flesh, angels can take on whatever form deemed most appropriate to ensure safe delivery of God's messages. Completely unselfish, totally pure, free from human constraints, angels exist for this purpose only: to guide us to serve Love.

Because angels are completely selfless and can only serve, humans cannot, as a general rule, become angels after physical death. Always learning, healing, growing, changing, we as humans walk a different path. Without question, human spirits can serve as guides for other humans, yet the essence of a human spirit differs from the stuff of which an angel is made.

As a medium, I am a messenger too. But I am not an angel. I love my fuzzy bathrobe, I don't play a harp, and I gave up on wearing white after having kids. Nonetheless, I deliver an important message from Source…: love survives physical death!

During my career as a spirit communicator, I have become aware that many of those affected by grief feel a great deal of uncertainty about what happens to their loved ones on the other side of this life. Near-death research aside, the afterlife remains, for many individuals, shrouded in impenetrable mysteries. With this level of uncertainty, those who are left behind when a loved one dies are often desperate for reassurance about the well-being of the loved one. The common cure for this type of dis-ease is what I call the "angelization" of those who have died.

Because angels are understood as being from God , always with God, loved by God, and kept by God, imagining that our departed loved ones become angels releases our own fears about life after death. If our loved ones are angels, they must be with God, so they must be in peace and guaranteed all the rights and privileges of heavenly splendor. But the truth is, no matter the label, regardless of the role, titles aside, we are all connected to God. Physical or non-physical, young or old, wild or mild, we are from God, always with God, loved by God, and kept by God.

Divine love is not just for angels. It is for *all*.

Bad People vs. Good People

I am often asked if "bad people" have the same outcome after death as those who have lived their lives in positive, loving ways. It's interesting to look at the word "outcome" in this sense. If so-called *bad people* have a different outcome, what would that look like? If they go to a different place – some far corner of the universe never to be heard from again – doesn't that sound a lot like the idea of hell? Most people who ask me this question are thinking in terms of the old-school heaven vs. hell idea, which separates bad people from good people.

But is there really such thing as a bad person? And if so, in a Christian theology, wouldn't the bad people deserve a chance to be healed and rehabilitated (forgiven)? The idea of eternal punishment is in direct conflict to the idea of divine forgiveness (healing), and therein lies a source of tremendous confusion for believers. Wouldn't it make more sense to believe that people who are severely wounded, sick and damaged need *help*, and that help is offered in the higher realms? I'm pretty sure that if souls are eternal, there are endless opportunities for this type of healing.

We are not here to strive for a conflict-free existence. That would defeat the whole purpose of incarnation. We are here to grow and stretch in response to conflict, so if growth is the outcome for a soul, then there can be no "bad" experiences or "bad" people, and certainly no eternal punishment. There are difficult, challenging and painful experiences of course, but they have a purpose, and they are all necessary to create expanded awareness and experiential balance. Like the positive and negative charges on a battery mentioned in Chapter Three, both are needed to make a complete connection.

Heaven and Hell

There is definitely a heaven, but it is a level of consciousness, not a remote location in the sky with gold-paved roads, pearly gates and a sky god sitting on a throne. And although the mere mention of the word "heaven" conjures up these images for many people, I think it's important for us to use the word in spiritual dialogs because it can actually help people shift their understanding of it. Once heaven is understood as a vibratory dimension (where we not only go when we die, but also when we dream, meditate or leave our bodies in other ways, such as unconsciousness or NDEs), the old imagery disappears, and the pain of grief can become a whole different experience.

It has become more common in popular culture recently for Bible-based Christians to come forward with stories about their near-death experiences. Two prime examples are Don Piper's book, *90 Minutes in Heaven*, and *Heaven is for Real*, a best-selling book written by the father (a pastor) of a boy who had a near-death experience at four years old. Both of these books describe Heaven in classic Sunday school fashion, with winged angels, Jesus, a heavenly choir and all the trimmings. Those of us who work in the in the field of afterlife studies are delighted to hear these stories, because it supports our work in two ways:

1. Traditionalists are beginning to acknowledge that of out-of-body journeying is possible.

2. These stories verify that we all see – initially – what we *expect* to see when we're temporarily dead.

It is important to remember that *all* near-death reports have one thing in common... the person came back to the physical world and did not stay dead. Therefore, these reports can only address the initial/early stages of death, because the person didn't go any further than the "greeting" process. There are a few exceptions in which experiencers report lengthy, detailed journeys into deeper levels of consciousness and timeless perspectives on the history of the universe, such as the remarkable account of Mellen Thomas Benedict.[53] But the garden variety NDE is rarely so comprehensive. Because most NDEers only visit the outer edges of the afterlife, the only way we can know what happens beyond that point is from what we learn through channeled messages and mediumship readings. Based on what we know from these messages (which tend to be very consistent), I think we can safely say that everybody is offered healing and love in the afterlife. Whether or not the help is immediately accepted is a matter of each individual's growth blueprint and soul journey.

Yes, there *are* reports of NDEs in which the person goes to a hellish-type place. But remember, that is just the entry phase. The person is working through fears, projections, guilt and other issues that need processing prior to moving fully into the light. This is part of a "life review" in which frightening negative experiences and emotions are examined and healed. It *can* be a terrifying process, depending on the material being reviewed, and hence, reports of visiting "hell." In fact, the whole concept of hell (and heaven) most likely originated from the reports of near-death experiencers in antiquity.

But these experiences are temporary, not eternal. This stage is well-known in Buddhism (the Tibetan Book of the Dead was created expressly for the purpose of guiding the dead through the various phases), and also known in ancient Egypt and many other cultures. I repeat... *It is temporary, not eternal.* And it is most certainly not foisted upon us by a judgmental god-in-the-sky. I'm pretty sure that no bona fide medium has ever brought in a message from a dead person saying, "I'm eternally burning in hell for my sins."

In the words of Austyn Wells, a noted Los Angeles medium, "In my experience, I have never had a soul talk about eternal damnation. However, they *do* acknowledge that there is great sadness about how we create a 'hellish' experience on earth. Quantum physics suggests that all moments are possible, and the spirit realm knows this to be true. Their wish for us is always that we set ourselves free from such limiting mental beliefs and step into the grander perspective that we are unlimited possibilities."

Christianity in its unfettered form (as the Gnostics saw it), and in fact most religions at their core, believe that we are beings of light temporarily embodied on earth, and that birth and death is a revolving door. All the extraneous dogma and doctrine that was heaped on top of that by the first and second century church organizers and evangelists pushed this true essence into a corner, and sadly, most people don't get to see it because they're too busy drinking the Kool Aid fed to them by church and culture.

But when we are in the throes of grief or trauma, the Kool Aid can seem woefully inadequate. Our hearts have been blown wide open, and in this vulnerable condition, we are actually more aligned with the divine than we are when we're walking around in our usual state of numbness. In this open place, the veil is very thin, so we can sense not only the presence of Spirit, but the presence of truth. If someone says, "Your son is going to Hell because he committed suicide," despite what you've been taught to believe, some part of you knows that this can't possibly be true, and you are faced with having to reconcile this conflict while also having to cope with your grief, which is a double burden, but also a double opportunity to expand your awareness.

Changing the Way We Look at Suicide

It is pointless to discuss grief, death and theology without including a discussion of suicide. Contrary to traditional notions of suicide as selfish or sinful, consider that throughout history, many cultures have seen value and honor in suicide under certain conditions, and it may be that we have something to learn from this idea. Perhaps it is just another form of conscious dying.

Historian and afterlife researcher Julia Assante PhD wrote in a recent blog that some suicides, such as those committed by people with life-threatening illnesses who are living with great suffering, are a form of conscious dying. She also identified a difference between those suicides and those of otherwise healthy people who can no longer tolerate the despair in their lives:

"In our present understanding, we define alive and dead materialistically, by the body's condition. In the future, I hope we will be wiser and understand that alive and dead transcend our materialist viewpoint and depend rather on an individual's state of consciousness. Because each of us decides inwardly how and when we will die, each of us commits suicide in a certain sense. Yet there is a difference. Those who take their own lives by shooting or hanging themselves, overdosing and the like are usually acting out of despair and self-hate. They have not solved the life problems they came here to work on. Nearly always, they bitterly regret their actions after death, and are shocked by the violence they inflicted on themselves."[54]

While it's true that readings from mediums consistently show that suicides experience what Assante describes, I would like to add the possibility that despair, regret and suicide is just as much a part of a soul's intention as a healthy, fulfilling "normal" life. Suicide is a very personal decision, and spiritually speaking, as painful as it is, it is part of the soul's growth trajectory, and also part of a learning curriculum for the other souls affected by the suicide. It is <u>never</u> useful to refer to someone who commits suicide as "selfish" or "sinful," because a judgment like that only perpetrates more pain and separation for everybody involved.

Someone who chooses suicide may actually be making a very evolved decision (on a soul level), contrary to how it might appear from the earth perspective. It is a decision to experience the ultimate act of judgment, which is judgment of the *self.* During earthly life we struggle with judgment all the time, but to rise up to the level of "un-judging" in any form, is an advanced program in earth school. A loved one who commits suicide is giving us the opportunity to practice un-judging on a grand scale. Remember, metaphysically speaking, we are all ONE, and we come here not as individuals, but as part of a collective consciousness with only one goal... to expand our awareness enough so that we can return to oneness and divine love. We come here not only to follow our own soul's path, but to support the paths of one another – of the collective. In that sense, many of the choices we make are a means of sponsoring the growth of others. Suicide is such a choice.

The idea of "choice" is understood differently in metaphysical terms, and is not the same thing we think of as choice in the earth realm. Even words like "deliberate" and "intentional" have very different meanings when we're looking at human experience from the perspective of the soul vs. the attachments and expectations of the ego body. Souls that create particularly difficult lesson plans, such as severe disabilities, addiction, depression or abuse, have highly developed souls that are seeking more powerful experiences that provide accelerated growth for themselves and the soul family members with whom they incarnate.

When someone chooses suicide, they are acting from a belief that there is no love available to them anywhere in the universe. It is an unimaginable loneliness, and is very much like the original wound of separation from Heaven when we first had the collective thought to live in human bodies. That first pang of icy wind, that sense of being out in the cold away from the warm house we just left, is shocking to the system, like diving into icy water. One who commits suicide feels something like this, and it is the ultimate act of judging one's experiences on earth. A suicidal person judges physical life *itself* as a bad experience, and opts out on the impetus of this thought.

Because we can't understand or relate to someone feeling that isolated and bereft, all we can do is focus on our own healing. The first step toward finding that healing is to un-judge the person and the act of suicide. Those who attempt – or succeed at – suicide need our love and compassion, not our judgment.

The choice of suicide is never an act committed *against* others. It is a uniquely personal and isolated decision that comes from deep pain that the rest of us can't possibly understand. The sooner we can release our suicided loved ones to their paths, the more healing we will find.

Because this is such a complicated and sensitive subject, I will insert here a channeled message about suicide from Danny on the Other Side (with the caveat that this is a somewhat esoteric spiritual teaching that may not be palatable to some readers):

Such a soul has chosen to work with judgment, and the choice to experience that level of ultimate judgment is a very bold choice. You have heard religion speak of *final judgment*, but you know that there is no external judge in the universe. Suicide is a form of final judgment, because it is a judgment one places on oneself; the self is the only true judge.

It is actually a very advanced lesson, not only for the person who kills himself, but for those who are affected by that event, because they are part of a soul group that has chosen to use that particular tool for growth.

The entire group experiences the idea of final judgment together. This is why when there is a massacre of innocents, such as a shooting at a school or a terrorist attack, there is an agreement between the beings involved that they will be affected and advanced, in some way, by one person's idea of self-judgment. The shooter or suicide bomber is experiencing this, and the others, on a soul level, have agreed to take a related piece of learning from that experience, but from a different vantage point.

At this level of understanding, one person in the scenario is not separate from another. All are interconnected, as equal and necessary parts of the expansion process. We all came in together, as one unified thought form, to assist each other on this shared journey. It is not 'independent study.' It is a cooperative classroom.

NOTES

[46] Vaughan-Lee, Llewellyn. *Sufism: The Transformation of the Heart*. Inverness, CA: Golden Sufi Center, 1995. Print. p. 45

[47] Marris, Peter. *Loss and Change*. New York: Pantheon, 1974. Print. p. 23

[48] qtd. in Archer, p. 115

[49] Rando, qtd. in Kastenbaum, Robert, Ph.D. Overview. n.d. Encyclopedia of Death. www.deathreference.com/Gi-Ho/Grief.html

[50] www.AfterlifeConference.com

[51] Giles, Jerry C. *The Encyclopedia of Mormonism*. Brigham Young University, The Harold B. Lee Library, n.d. Web. 31 Dec. 2013. <http://eom.byu.edu/index.php/Angels>.

[52] www.AngelsInSight.com

[53] http://mellen-thomas.com/

[54] Assante, Julia, PhD, "Conscious Dying or Suicide: What Is the Difference?" *The Last Frontier*. www.juliaassante.com/conscious-dying-or-suicide-what-is-the-difference

7. Oneness vs. Twoness

"Mysticism... is an encounter of such immensity that everything else shifts in position. Mystics have no need to exclude or eliminate others, precisely because they have experienced radical inclusivity of themselves into something much bigger. They do not need to define themselves as enlightened or superior, whereas a mere transfer of religious assertions often makes people even more elitist and more exclusionary. True mystics are glad to be common, ordinary, servants of all, and 'just like everybody else,' because any need for specialness has been met once and for all."

Richard Rohr [55]

What kind of "specialness" is Rohr talking about here? To me, the idea of specialness is usually a cosmic joke that endlessly loops back on itself, because once we become aware of oneness, we realize that as part of the boundless cosmic soup, there *is* no specialness anywhere in the universe. At the same time, when we realize that we are not separate from the divine or from each other, we walk around with a secret smile; an inner knowing that confirms without a doubt that everything is occurring exactly as it should. While that kind of knowingness can certainly feel special, the joke is that it actually strips us of our illusion of specialness.

Understanding oneness vs. twoness (also known as duality vs. non-duality), can dramatically shift the way we experience grief and loss. If we understand that we are not separate from anything else in the universe, from the tiniest adamantine particle to entire solar systems, it changes the way we look at our relationships. In oneness, mother and son, husband and wife, perpetrator and victim no longer exist as identifiers of what we are to one another. In fact, at this level of understanding, there *are* no others. There is no "them vs. us." There is only *us*. Nothing is separate from anything else.

So how does this relate to grief and loss?

For some bereaved individuals (as evidenced by the Facebook comments that inspired this book), losses are inextricably tied to anger and blame. In their view of how the universe operates, there has to be someone or something at fault, whether it's the drunk driver who caused the accident, the doctor who misdiagnosed the disease, or the god that didn't live up to its imagined promise of safety and protection. Within this structure we find what *A Course in Miracles* calls "special relationships," a form of attachment and identification that keeps us from seeing ourselves as equal with every other piece in the kaleidoscope, and makes loss more difficult to understand and accept. If you aren't familiar with *A Course in Miracles,* a bit of interpretation may be in order. When they refer to "Holy Spirit," they are speaking of the conduit that connects us directly to divine source, which is our natural state of awareness. It can also be interpreted as our willingness to trust the flow, to listen to our inner voice and to relinquish our notions of how things "should" be. With that in mind, consider the following *Course in Miracles* teaching about special relationships:[56]

"The special relationships of the world are destructive, selfish, and childishly egocentric. Yet, if given to the Holy Spirit, these relationships can become the holiest things on earth—the miracles that point the way to the return to Heaven. The world uses its special relationships as a final weapon of exclusion and a demonstration of separateness. The Holy Spirit transforms them into perfect lessons in forgiveness and in awakening from the dream. Each one is an opportunity to let perceptions be healed and errors corrected. Each one is another chance to forgive oneself by forgiving the other. And each one becomes still another invitation to the Holy Spirit and to the remembrance of God... Forgiveness is the means by which we will remember. Through forgiveness the thinking of the world is reversed. The forgiven world becomes the gate of Heaven, because by its mercy we can at last forgive ourselves. Holding no one prisoner to guilt, we become free."

Imagine applying this wisdom to a grief experience in which no one is held prisoner to guilt, not even ourselves. All is accepted, forgiven and released. We realize that we're all on the wheel together, united by a common intention to become saturated by love as we come to recognize our role as divine sparks on a shared journey. All those we blame – the doctor, the drunk driver or the punitive god – are teachers, partners and journey-sharers.

That is Oneness.

Many Mansions

Within the Oneness are countless levels and realms, and I believe this is the meaning of the Christian teaching, "In my father's house are many mansions." The mansions are levels of awareness. They are a limitless network of connecting fibers that contain and transmit the collective visions, experiences, creations and projections of every soul (animal, mineral or vegetable). These mansions are infinite and impossible to count. They are universes upon universes upon universes, and they are all connected. If we narrow down the focus to our earthly existence, all our experiences – joyful or tragic – are like rooms inside the many mansions. In fact, they are like corners in the rooms in the mansions, or dust in the corners of the rooms, or specks in the dust in the corners of the rooms, or cells inside the specks in the dust, which contain a billion more universes within them... and so on into infinity. In this picture, our personal dramas seem very small.

This scenario triggers a lot of questions. What's the purpose of our experiences? If we are just particles in a universe of cosmic dust bunnies, do our experiences have any meaning? What is the purpose of our attachments, losses, pain and grief? Is the whole thing limited to just one short, egocentric physical life span in which we only end up dying and dissolving into oblivion?

I cannot claim to have the definitive answers, but I do know – and strongly believe – what I have received intuitively through my channeling work. Without apology, I will share that here, even though it might alienate some of the more academic-minded readers among you, because nothing I am going to say can be proven scientifically or understood with the rational mind.

We create our experiences in order to contribute to the One Consciousness. It is as if we are filling a library with all the accumulated experience in all of creation, because this library is the source of *everything*. You may know it as *The Akashic Record*. It is, in a sense, our home base. Our mothership. When our physical bodies die, or when we go into deep meditation or dream states, we don't just float aimlessly in space. We go *home*, to the library, to share and receive information. That's what dreams and visions are. That's the source tapped into by mediums, psychics, healers and channelers. It's where art, music, literature, theology, philosophy and technology come from. It is a great depository for all our creations.

The experiences we have on earth are our contributions to the library. We are constantly mining information to educate and nurture the collective, and we do this with great love, because it is our prime directive. It is the reason we chose to come to earth in the first place; to feed the collective like worker bees supporting a hive. Our choice to do this was an enormous commitment – perhaps a sacrifice –when we originally decided to separate from Oneness to experience physicality.

But don't take my word for it. Study the deeper mystical teachings of any religion and you will find Oneness there. The ancient Gnostic Christians, in their telling of the creation of the universe, describe "the father" (creator) perceiving its own image within its own light, and that act of perception – the awareness of itself– creates a split from itself, resulting in twoness.[57] The story of Adam and Eve being rejected from the garden is a metaphor for the same split (only in that story, guilt, evil and punishment were added to the narrative).

But when the narrative is stripped away, what we find is a common thread that describes creation as simply the "densification" of light and sound into matter (my friend Barry describes it as the "sound" of the Big Bang). The Hindus knew about sound and light way before anybody in the west attempted to describe it, hence the colors of the chakras and the practice of chanting. And shamans have worked with the electromagnetic fields of plants and animals for eons. The early Christian communities knew this too, which is why the Aramaic translation of what most people know in Greek/English as "The Lord's Prayer" says:

"Oh Thou, from whom the breath of life comes, who fills all realms of sound, light and vibration. May your light be experienced in my utmost holiest. Your Heavenly Domain approaches. Let Your will come true - in the universe (all that vibrates) just as on earth (that is material and dense).[58]

We *all* know this innately, but once we incarnate into the dense stuff of physical matter, we tend to forget. The spiritual quest is about trying to find our way back to it. When grief opens our hearts, this memory has an opportunity to grab our attention and remind us of our relationship to the Light. When we're grieving, our wounds feel like gaping holes in our being, but they are not holes... they are *openings*.

NOTES

[55] Rohr, Richard. *Following the Mystics Through the Narrow Gate... Seeing God in All Things* (CD, DVD, MP3)
[56] http://acim.org/AboutACIM/what_it_says.html
[57] Davies, Stevan L. *The Secret Book of John: The Gnostic Gospel Annotated & Explained*. Woodstock, VT: SkyLight Paths Pub., 2005. Print. Pp 21,22
[58] http://www.thenazareneway.com/lords_prayer.htm

8. Love Beyond Life: From Grief to Belief

"Death may be the greatest of all human blessings."
Socrates

In 1974 when I was a 21 year-old hippie hitchhiking across America, hanging out in communes and ingesting psychedelic substances, I found an image in a science magazine that took my breath away. I cut it out of the magazine, taped it onto the front page of my personal journal, and added the caption, "Living in Learnful Effect of Everything."

Today, 40 years later, a colorized version of this image serves as the logo for my non-profit organization, *The Afterlife Education Foundation*. The image dazzles everybody who looks at it, because it speaks volumes about the multi-dimensional existence that is available to us if we're willing to look for it. I knew this to be true when I was young, and I know it even more now.

115

In Chapter Five I talked about how some bereavement groups refuse to allow discussion of after-death communication. While these groups offer a valuable service in the form a community where bereaved people can share their stories and their suffering, without an open forum for exploring a diverse array of options for healing, the suffering people wander aimlessly in a maze with no way out. To deny this exploration to a grieving person disrespects the sacred process of grieving. It is counterproductive and contrary to the healing process.

Without being open to the possibility that there are dimensions beyond the physical realm – a realm with which we are so familiar and overly-identified -- we are missing out on our true potential. Just like the character in the image that inspired me so much in 1974, we can choose to look beyond the curtain or to stay entrenched behind it. We can cower in fear and cling to the narrow definition of reality given to us by church, state and corporation, or we can open our minds and ask for more. That is the true meaning of "seek and ye shall find."

After working with thousands of bereaved people over the last several years, I've observed that the hard-core materialist/science-minded people suffer the most in grief. I'm referring to those who believe that after death, consciousness is simply obliterated. There is no more existence, no real point to life or death, nothing but a short span of physical life and then NOTHING. Consciousness simply flickers out and disappears, because in this view, consciousness is inextricably tied to the body, so when the body goes, *everything* goes. From what I've observed (and this is not a scientific statement, just a personal and professional observation), people who believe this seem to have the most difficult time dealing with loss and grief, more difficult even than those who are afraid of hell.

A friend recently sent me an article by Rabbi Marc Gellman explaining why clergy should oppose mediumship.[60] In the article Gellman states, "There are two basic reasons why every major religious tradition does not believe in consulting people who say they can speak to the dead. First, most mediums are fakes, and second, trying to contact the dead is a bad spiritual idea."

That's a very strong statement, and it begs for spirited debate. I would hope that this rabbi, as an educated man, would be able to support his position with an intelligent argument. But the arguments he poses are absurd. He says, "The fake medium says in effect, 'Death is not real because it does not really cut off your ability to communicate with your loved one.'"

Is that what *fake* mediums say? Because *real* mediums say the same thing, as do spiritual teachers, near-death experiencers, prophets from most religious traditions and a good number of doctors, hospice nurses, grief counselors and scientists.

I don't know what Rabbi Gellman's personal beliefs are, but since Judaism doesn't really address life after death in any substantial way, I'm going to guess that he doesn't believe that a soul or some sort of essence survives bodily death. As for mediums telling us that death isn't "real," what they're actually saying is that death *as the absolute end of consciousness* isn't real. That's a big difference, though as always, semantics gets in the way, because what exactly is the definition of "real" anyway? And while we're at it, what is the definition of "death?"

Gellman disapproves of mediums offering the possibility that death isn't what we think it is and that communication with the dead is possible. But how does he know this isn't true? Has he ever had a reading with a reputable medium? Has he reviewed the academic research of Dr. Gary Schwartz, Dr. Stuart Hameroff or Dr. Julie Beischel?

Probably not.

Sure there are fakes out there, just like there are quack gynecologists, corrupt Wall Street tycoons and con artists of every ilk. Rabbi Gelman goes on to say, "The medium pretends to provide ways to deny death. This is not just a cruel deception; it can also be an obstacle to a person's grief work."

This would certainly be true if the medium in question is a fake, but apparently, even if a medium is real and the reading is accurate, Gellman still thinks it's a bad idea, because he believes "We do better when certain spiritual barriers are not breached, and the main barrier erected by God is the barrier between life and death."

Gellman says in the article (and Jewish tradition agrees), "When we are alive, this world of the living ought to be our main focus."

Does this mean that we should *not* ponder non-earthly things? If so, then religion and spirituality in general is a bad idea, since the ancient mystics, sages and prophets, including today's monks, rabbis and priests, would be wasting their time thinking about other worlds. According to Gellman, God intends for the barrier between life and death to be imponderable and impenetrable. He even describes near-death experiences (NDEs) as "an understandable but religiously misguided attempt to make religion scientific."

He obviously didn't bother to consult the vast body of bona-fide scientific research that exists about NDEs. Nor did he bother to consult his own religious tradition. If he really wanted to make a religious case against mediums, he would have quoted the standard Biblical fallback position, Deuteronomy 18:10-12:

"Let no one be found among you who sacrifices their son or daughter in the fire, who practices divination or sorcery, interprets omens, engages in witchcraft, or casts spells, or who is a medium or spiritist or who consults the dead. Anyone who does these things is detestable to the LORD; because of these same detestable practices the LORD your God will drive out those nations before you."

Yes, it's in the old (Hebrew) testament. But Gellman didn't mention it at all, even though this passage is the primary reason why most Christians and Jews are afraid to communicate with the spirit world (even though their prophets and saints did it all the time). Practicing divination was considered evil enough to be compared to throwing sons and daughters into a fire, but apparently it was perfectly acceptable for Hebrew prophets like Abraham, Moses and Elijah, and New Testament heroes like Mary, Joseph, Paul and many others, not to mention the sainted visionaries who came later.

So where does all this fear come from?

To answer this question, I refer again to the wisdom of Dr. Julia Assante, who is an expert in near-eastern literature and history. She tells us that most of our fear of death is rooted in early Judaism, based on the idea that human beings were created to be immortal. According to the creation myth, Eve ruined that for us by bringing "sin" into the world, which resulted in death being meted out as punishment rather than a natural end of physical life. With death as a penalty for disobedience, no wonder it is so feared by those who take biblical mythology literally.

Assante explains:

"The ambiguity in the Bible around survival after death... worsened considerably with the reforms of King Josiah in the 7th century BCE, a time when the Yahweh cult was refashioned to fit monarchy. Under Josiah, mourning rites were curtailed and communication with the dead, a practice that was common for millennia in every household throughout the ancient Near East, was outlawed. Anyone caught practicing necromancy was stoned to death. The chief reason was because the dead were referred to as *Elohim*, a word that means "gods" [plural]. The living believed that people gained wisdom and even special powers after death and looked to their dead family members for help as we do today. Such a belief undermined people's dependency on the one God and their devotion to him. With the criminalization of afterlife communication, the living's access to the afterlife was closed. The dead could no longer speak, so became effectively nonexistent. We are only now beginning to turn this around."

So now that we know where the fear of death and after-death communication comes from (at least in Western culture), how do we begin to bridge the gap between superstitious terror and an open conduit to other dimensions that can help us find peace and healing in our lives?

We begin by changing the way we look at time and space.

When we are receiving intuitive messages, or dreaming, or in deep meditation, we are transcending the rational, mundane earth mind, which exists in a three-dimensional universe where space and time appear to move from Point A to Point B in a more or less straight line. But spiritual interactions take place in a dimension that doesn't receive, organize or record data the same way the body/mind does. When we are receiving, or *intuiting*, we are completely in present time. Almost everybody has experienced a fleeting sense of "time standing still" at some point in their lives; a feeling of being "spaced out" or drifting away. These moments are usually eerie and surreal, and they tend to pass quickly. They are a glimpse into another level of consciousness, but our egos cling so desperately to the familiar that we are quickly yanked back to this reality where everything is safe and predictable.

Recognizing timelessness is one of the greatest gifts we can receive, and sometimes, rather than experiencing it through consciousness-expanding practices like meditation or psychotropic substances, we are forced into a sense of timelessness as the result of trauma and shock. This explains why many people receive visits from departed loved ones very soon after the death occurs, because the bereaved person is in an open, timeless state (this same thing happens to a person who is dying and traveling back and forth between dimensions).

In the dimension we normally occupy on earth, we believe that somebody has to be somewhere else in order for communication to be achieved. A distance has to be bridged. A gap has to be closed. I have to call out to you across a room, or dial your phone number, or whisper in your ear or send you an email in order to communicate with you. I have to be *here* and you have to be *there*. There has to be some sort of gap between us, because we think that space/time exists in a straight line, from here to there, with a space in-between.

But imagine that there *is* no space in-between. No "there." Imagine that everything is *here,* now, in the here and now. That's what non-linear time looks like. If everything is here now, then nothing can ever really "end" because it's always *here now,* so all it can do is change energetic form. In order to open ourselves to communication with the other side, we must understand and accept this completely. That is what the great mystics mean when they talk about *faith.* They are talking about our awareness of – and our trust in – our innate relationship to the non-physical universe.

That trust is *everything.* In terms of communicating with our loved ones on the Other Side, if we get too caught up in worrying that we're not hearing from them, or that they're distant and not sending us messages, our trust will be compromised and the conduit will close.

A few years ago I found myself so swept up in the world of academia and the intellect that I started neglecting my meditations, rituals and spiritual practices, and I felt that the communications I'd previously been receiving from my guides and my son on the Other Side had stopped cold. But a wonderful teacher/friend gave me a fantastic analogy that helped me understand what was happening. She told me to think of myself as the ocean and the world of spirit as the moon. Does the ocean worry when it can't see the moon on a cloudy night? Does it say, "Where is the moon?" The ocean may be busy moving with the pull of the earth, but it knows it is always connected to the moon, even when the moon isn't visible.

Making Contact with the Dead

It's far easier to connect with the Other Side than most people think. Movies and literature have given us the expectation that we should be able to see the dead with our physical senses (hearing their voices, seeing them in bodily form, smelling their perfume), when it is actually our *non-physical* senses that engage with other dimensions. The expectation of physical evidence actually prevents a lot of people from making contact, because they're looking through the wrong lens. I've seen many bereaved people suffer because they feel that they aren't getting any messages, when in fact they're getting messages all the time, but simply don't recognize them.

The evidence we're looking for, and the language in which other dimensions speak to us, is energetic rather than physical. It is more about feeling a presence or sensing an idea *internally* than experiencing something *external* like words or pictures. Energetic messages from the higher realms don't originate in human language. They are signals that could be compared to electrical impulses. Our brains receive these signals, and then translate them into forms we can understand. When we receive these signals, they go through our earthly filters, so it makes sense that in near-death experiences, Christians might see Jesus, very young children might see Disney characters, some of us will see departed loved ones, while someone else might experience white light, pink light, a tunnel, angels or some other translation of the energy being transmitted. In other words, the messages originate in Spirit are something akin to "electrical" signals (I often describe these signals as bleeps and blips, or white noise), and our physical brains translate those signals into words and pictures. So if a medium is bringing in a message from a man wanting to tell his widow that he loves her, he might send a pink rose, because that was her favorite flower and it will convince her that he's really there. His consciousness knows that she will understand this symbol, so he creates it energetically. A skilled medium who connects to the consciousness of both the sender and the receiver will translate it accurately. It's all energy. The forms are just symbols that communicate that energy.

When we "see" our dead loved ones in the form they had in physical life, our brains are creating those images because it helps us identify who the person is. Once we get more skilled at receiving messages, we can identify the person without attaching the image of a body, and recognize them just by the feeling of their energy. Most of us get our messages through dreams and symbols, but there are several different "clair senses" that can be used, such as clairvoyance (seeing images), clairaudience (hearing sounds or words), and other receptive senses that include clairsentience (bodily sensations), clairscent (smelling), clairtangency (picking up messages through touching an object), clairgustance (picking up message through taste) clairempathy (sensing an emotion related to someone on The Other Side), and channeling.[61]

If you take nothing else from the previous paragraphs, remember this... we came to earth with our connection to Source/Oneness completely intact, and we are designed to *stay* connected. It isn't a special gift. It is a birthright

To a Soul, Forgiveness is NOT Optional

Your soul is what you were (and still are) before you separated from Oneness. It is *your essence,* without the identification of yourself as John Smith, a librarian from Paoli Indiana and the father of two great kids, or Elizabeth Taylor, a beautiful movie star. To your soul, those identities are merely props that help move you forward in your curriculum so you can contribute the experiences of that identity to the collective.

Our incarnate identities are like costumes donned temporarily to act out the roles of different characters, and our incarnations are like attending a series of costume parties. All the people at these parties are members of our soul family, and it's as if we go from party to party, always wearing a different costume. For example, in the incarnation I most recently shared with my son, he dressed as a seriously ill child and I dressed as his mother (along with numerous other identities, characteristics and sub plots, of course). In our past incarnations we might have worn the costumes of brother and sister, or husband and wife, or slave and master. But in the greater picture, in the view of Oneness, we create stories designed to generate the wisdom that enables us to do our best work in each role (each incarnation). It is a delightful little game, and the soul rejoices in it. Along the way in these incarnations, we sometimes experience horrendous, incomprehensible, unimaginable suffering. And that's where forgiveness and timelessness enters the picture.

The understanding of timelessness is one of the most important elements in learning to un-judge, forgive and release attachments. If there is no time – if there is no time *limit* – then opportunities for healing are endless. Because most of us think of time as linear and limited, we think we must wrap everything up before we "die." But if we don't die, and the soul continues to acquire experience forever, then there is literally all the time in the world to heal, release and forgive. The costume parties and the characters keep recurring with a continuous thread of energy seeking to be healed or balanced. Because we have all the time in the world to work with these energies, and the ultimate goal is healing and balance, then forgiveness (which really means releasing our attachment to negative experiences) *isn't optional*. Forgiveness (releasing) is the whole point!

When you look at the parties and the costumes from the perspective of timelessness, you will see that they are constantly shifting and restructuring, like the fragments in a kaleidoscope. But they never *end*, because the concept of ending requires a belief in linear time. Without time, the kaleidoscope just keeps turning for eternity, and the energy accumulated through all that movement becomes integrated into the whole of creation. This is the true meaning of karma; it is never good or bad, and is certainly never about reward or punishment. It is simply *the evolution of creation,* and all the experiences in creation are purposeful and necessary. When this is realized, it becomes possible to "un-judge" our experiences, to release ourselves and others from blame, and to understand forgiveness in a new way.

Most souls are completely self-aware after they leave the physical body, and they are delighted when they see that the whole plan – spanning all their incarnations – can be understood. It all begins to make sense, and the journey to this awareness has a tremendous amount of momentum. Whatever is going on at the earth level, such as the grieving, anger or guilt of loved ones, may be a distraction for the departed soul for a short period of time, but it is not strong enough to alter the momentum of a soul's path. A soul entering the higher realms is met by teachers, guides, angels, ancestors and loved ones who help it move forward through a process that begins with what is commonly known as a "life review." It could be compared to presenting a PhD dissertation at the end of one's post-graduate studies.

There is healing to do, forgiveness work, fragments of traumas, emotional baggage and other imprints to process, but this is done with the help of unconditionally-loving healers and teachers in heaven. Sometimes there is struggle and resistance, and the process can be painful, hence the depictions of torment in "hell," which are based on reports from near-death experiencers who came back to their bodies before they could fully integrate into the light of healing.

For grievers who worry that their sadness will hold their loved ones back from the light, know that the pull toward spiritual healing is much stronger than the desire to hang around the dense, dark energy of sadness, anger and guilt on earth. The best thing a bereaved person can do for their departed loved one is to work on letting go of the heavy energy of their own anger and guilt. We cannot hold our loved ones back from their journeys. They are light and free.

We are the ones stuck in darkness.

NOTES

[59] From French artist and astronomer Nicolas Camille Flammarion (1842-1925). Flammarion authored more than 50 titles on science, astronomy and spiritism. This piece, entitled *Other Worlds* first appeared in his 1888 edition of *L'Atmosphère.*
[60] Gellman, Marc. "God Squad: Why Clergy Oppose Mediums." *God Squad: Why Clergy Oppose Mediums*. Newsday.com, 2 Jan. 2014. Web. 02 Jan. 2014. <www.newsday.com/columnists/god-squad/god-squad-why-clergy-oppose-mediums-1.6710765>.
[61] http://www.quantumpossibilities.biz/clairs.htm

9. Rituals: Turning Pain into Power

"The grief in the human heart needs to be attended to by rituals and practices that when practiced, will lessen anger and allow creativity to flow anew."

Matthew Fox

"Ritual gives words to the unspeakable and form to the formless. It brings the non-physical into physical form so we can see it, touch it, feel it and process it. Creating this link between Heaven and Earth helps us to see the connection clearly, and to establish a bond between the realms, which gives us great comfort. It brings the spirit of the dead person into the body of the grieving person, and closes the perceived gap between them."

Terri Daniel

Most of us go through our lives more or less numb and basically asleep. Even when grief offers us an opening for awakening, we often don't recognize it or act on it because death and grief are such taboo topics in our society. In the five years since I wrote about ritual in my last book, I have studied and practiced rituals from a variety of world spiritual traditions, and have learned a lot about the healing power of ceremony.

The Native American family described in Chapter Five gave us a beautiful example of how to access wisdom and intimacy when facing the absolute certainty of death. They brought rituals and clear intention to the death of their family matriarch, and in my chaplaincy work I've seen this happen with spiritually-oriented people from all traditions, whether Buddhist, Jewish, Christian, Muslim, Pagan or anything else. Deathbed and funeral rituals helped them walk directly *with* the death rather than shrinking away from it. By contrast, I have also observed people with an "in-name-only" spirituality (or no spirituality at all), who have no symbolic implements to help them work with loss or trauma.

If I compare the two families described in Chapter Five, the Native Americans used their spirituality (sacred objects, chanting, drumming and prayers) and its cultural practices (crying and grieving openly and taking the body home for burial), as guideposts for walking through the experience of death and grief. The other family – the one with the angry son, no spiritual beliefs and no plans for any kind of memorial service – had none of these tools. Instead, they projected their pain and anger outward by suing the hospital.

In the summers of 2007 and 2008 I volunteered at a bereavement camp for children who had lost a loved one. Many of the campers had experiences that were dreadful beyond imagining. One eight year-old told me about witnessing his mother's suicide by gunshot, and another boy, age 11, told me that after his father's murder, his mother, grandmother and other family members would not tell him what happened, only that his father had died. He eventually heard the details from the other kids at school, who had heard it from *their* parents.

There were dozens of stories like this, and in most cases the children were not given adequate or accurate information about the deaths, nor did they receive grief counseling or any viable help for dealing with the experience. For almost all the children, the camp was the first opportunity they had to talk openly about the experience and to participate in rituals specifically designed to help facilitate the expression of their grief.

One such ritual involved helping the children make "memory boats" out of large pieces of bark decorated with moss, twigs, flowers, feathers and scraps of paper on which they could write messages to their departed loved ones. We then set the little boats adrift on the river as a visual expression of releasing and letting go.

Another ritual was facilitated by a dance therapist who led the kids in a movement process that expressed characteristics of the departed parent. In this exercise, the children stood in a circle taking turns mimicking a physical movement that the parent commonly used, such as casting a fly fishing line, smoking a cigarette or mixing cake batter in a bowl. These were significant visual impressions the children remembered about their dead parents, and by bringing these memories to the surface and physically acting them out, the essence of the parent expressed itself through the body of the child.

Creative rituals like these are designed to open the heart and a conduit to the divine as a path to healing. But they don't have to be limited to an organized grief group or structured spiritual practice. They can be done at home quite easily, on your own or with the help of a friend, and they don't have to be tied to any particular religion, culture or belief system. They can be sacred or secular, formal or casual, reverent or light-hearted. They can be done just once, or every year on a milestone date, or whenever you feel the need to connect more deeply. They are a form of meditation, and unless you are following a specifically-prescribed religious ritual, there are really no rules.

For example, last month I helped a friend do a sacred ceremony for a house she's selling. Her young son died in that house two years earlier after a long battle with cancer, and she had just moved to a new house. The old house was all cleaned up, vacant and ready to sell, but she struggled emotionally with letting go of the only home her son had ever known. So we did a "releasing ceremony" in the old house. We carried incense from room to room, summoning her son's spirit – along with all our guides, angels, teachers and loved ones in the higher realms – and asked them to help us clear the house of any negativity, fear and pain that remained there. It was very emotional as my friend led me from room to room, talking about her son's life and the memories held in this house. We both cried as we opened up to the pain of loss, but our tears mixed with laughter as we felt the energetic lifting of that pain. We soon realized that the energy we were working to release was not held inside the house... it was held inside the mother's heart.

The same mother had a very large collection of her young son's drawings (he was quite the little artist). When she moved to the new house, she had to choose which drawings to keep and which to let go of. But how do we let go of such precious items? We can give some of them away to special friends, but we can't just throw the remainder in the recycling bin, because they are sacred objects and should be treated as such. The answer is *ritual*. My friend decided to take herself to the coast for a retreat, and while there, burn the drawings in a ceremonial bonfire on the beach.

Rituals like this help us move from the attachments of the ego-body into a more spacious, soul-level awareness. They remind us that grieving doesn't have to be all misery, all the time. There are countless ways to lighten the burden for a few small moments here and there, and ritual is one of many tools we have at our disposal. With the regular use of ritual, those pain-free moments when we experience a glimpse of timelessness can become more frequent, until we can recognize and honor our pain when it calls for our attention, but then let it go when our full attention is *not* required.

I've written a lot about rituals over the years, so I don't want to repeat old material, but I've put together the following list of creative rituals that can help us move consciously and openly through the grief process. One of my favorite (but more complex) grieving rituals is the *Aya Despacho,* a Shamanic ceremony that involves creating a bundle of sacred materials such as stones, colored paper, herbs and other symbolic, sacred objects to create a "rainbow bridge between the worlds, to ease the process of crossing over," as described by my shaman friend and teacher, Kitty Edwards.[62] Once this bundle is assembled, it is burned in a fire to represent non-attachment to the outcome and a release of all claims to that which was given away. It is a very powerful ritual that we teach at our annual Afterlife Conference.[63]

In *Embracing Death* I included a long list of practical meaningful rituals for coping with grief. But here, I'd like to add some new ones that are specifically designed for allowing grief to move through us and guide us on our transformative journeys. Many thanks to the friends and followers who contributed some of these ideas:

The Family Quilt

Sarah's husband died from a heart attack at age 56. The pain of cleaning out his closet and getting rid of his clothes was too much to bear, until a friend suggested that she make a quilt from her husband's shirts. She hired a local quilter, and the result was a gorgeous quilt that she wrapped herself up in every night. Five years later Sarah married again, and the quilt was handed down to her daughter, who used it for her brand new baby. Life goes on and on, and the spirit of Sarah's husband was honored to welcome that beautiful little grandchild soul.

Ashes to Ashes... and to Everything Else

If your loved one was cremated, instead of scattering the ashes all at one time in one place, consider scattering *some* of them and keeping the rest to use in future rituals, such as the person's death anniversary (transition day) or birthday. Sprinkle the ashes in your garden or into a river every year on this milestone date, or use them to create art in some form. When I built my house in 2007, I put some of my son's ashes in each of the four corners of my property to create sacred space. You can do this every time you move to a new house, or every season when you plant a new garden. It's all about *renewal.* It is also possible to have the cremains used in blown glass art objects, and even in tattoos!

Every Home Needs an Altar

People from a wide range of religious traditions create altars in their homes, whether they're dedicated to Mary and Jesus, Vishnu, the Great Spirit or departed loved ones and ancestors. An altar can be a small table in a corner of any room, and on it, you can place anything you like that connects you to Spirit or the essence of your loved ones on the Other Side. Photos of the person, some of their personal sacred objects, healing stones, flowers, hand-written messages... anything at all. Light candles on this altar whenever you feel moved to connect. It can be a yearly birthday or transition day, or *every* day, as you see fit.

Home for the Holidays

Many grievers find birthdays, Thanksgiving and the winter holidays a time of great sadness because their loved ones aren't present in physical form. But instead of focusing on their absence, consider focusing on their presence by inviting them to the festivities. This is not such a bizarre idea when you consider that Christians use the symbolism of bread and wine to represent the flesh and blood of Jesus, and Jews set a place for the prophet Elijah at the Passover table each year. On birthdays, bake your loved one's favorite cake and gather friends for an "earth birthday" celebration (if your friends think you're crazy for doing this, it's time to find new friends). On Thanksgiving, light a candle for your loved one, and have everybody at the table share a special memory of him or her. On Christmas, decorate your tree with the special ornaments that were meaningful to that person. Don't hide from those memories and feelings. They are more easily healed and balanced when we invite them in rather than shoo them away.

Get Out of Town
Was your departed beloved crazy about golf vacations in the Caribbean, dude ranches in Texas or art museums in Italy? If you have the resources to do so, follow his or her footsteps on your next vacation. You might be surprised at what you find there.

Read Books and Listen to Lectures on the Afterlife, and Develop a Mediation Practice to Help You Connect
Read everything you can get your hands on. Have readings with reputable mediums. Attend our annual afterlife conference. Start becoming your own conduit. The first book I always recommend is *Opening to Channel* by Sanaya Roman. You can find it on Amazon.

Get the kids and grandkids involved
Teach them about the departed. They can write letters to grandpa, add objects to the altar, or share their dreams and visions. Invite them to draw pictures or write stories about the loved one, or better yet, encourage them to talk about their views of death and other worlds. If they are really suffering, please, ask your local hospice for referrals to grief groups, camps and other resources for children. The worst thing you can do for grieving children is to isolate them from the process.

As I complete the final edit of this book, I find myself guided to include the rituals I mentioned in my previous book, *Embracing Death*, because this section seems incomplete without them:

Create a Journey Blanket

If you have a loved one who is dying, consider creating a memorial quilt or "journey blanket" for him or her. Eighteen months before my son died, I gathered a group of friends in my living room for a potluck dinner and a quilting bee. Each person brought a piece of fabric that had special meaning to them, and these – along with pieces of fabric from Danny's own life – were cobbled into a beautiful patchwork quilt, filled with love, prayers and blessings. It was far from technically perfect, with sloppy stitching and uneven squares, but the energy it held was magical. The quilt was very warm and Danny slept with it for the next two winters. The following summer he died lying on top of that quilt, and now I sleep and meditate with it, and it has become *my* journey blanket also.

Get a Tattoo

Many of the firefighters who battled the blaze at the World Trade Center on September 11, 2001 felt unbearable grief and guilt about the partners who'd fought beside them and perished. Some of them processed and ritualized their grief by having images of their fallen friends tattooed on their backs. The firefighters said, "This way I will have my partner's spirit with me every day of my life." When I heard about this, I asked Danny (11 years old at the time) what animal he would be if he could choose to be one. He chose a swan, and the following week I had a tattoo of a swan on my left shoulder.

Locks of Love

In the days leading up to my son's death, while he was in and out of consciousness, I often sat beside him stroking his thick, beautiful hair. One day I realized that locks of his hair would make extraordinary gifts for the people who loved him. So with his permission, I snipped small pieces and tied each with a delicate red ribbon. I've given them all away except for the one I kept for myself.

Put it in a Locket
I keep a tiny snippet of that hair in a heart-shaped locket that I wear almost every day.

Open the Treasure Chest and Give the Riches Away
When you're ready to start going through your departed loved one's possessions, think of it as a sacred rite of passage. Invite friends to help, and light candles, say prayers, open a bottle of champagne and share memories, stories, laughter and tears as you look through the precious objects. Set aside selected items to give to friends as remembrance tokens, or make something wonderful and creative out of them. One of my friends made pillowcases from her mother's antique tablecloths.

Hold Court
If the dying person is open to it and is physically able, she can choose which belongings she'd like to give to friends and family members. When my friend Betty was dying, she asked her sons to display her special possessions around the house. She was a collector of healing crystals, and the dining room table was covered with magnificent geodes, quartz obelisks, rare stones and other sacred objects. Her friends were invited to take whatever pieces called out to them, with Betty's full participation and blessing. She even chose to have her memorial service while she was still alive. Friends gathered at her house to tell heartwarming stories about their experiences with Betty, light candles, sing songs and recite beautiful prayers and readings. Betty's bed was moved into the living room for the occasion, and she sat there regally, beaming with happiness.

Plant a Tree or a Memorial Garden
If you can't plant a tree or shrub in a public place in honor of your loved one, create a special corner of your yard as a memorial garden. Plant special trees and flowers there, and decorate the space with pictures, sacred objects, religious icons

or anything that inspires you. If your loved one was cremated, this is an excellent place to sprinkle some of the ashes.

Send your Loved One on a World Tour

There are many creative and meaningful ways to use cremation ashes (also known as "cremains") in ceremony, and the ceremonies do not have to be formal or somber. Because my son loved to travel, I divided some of his ashes into tiny, decorated bottles and gave one to each of our closest friends to carry with them on their vacations and business trips. His ashes have now been sprinkled in at least a dozen countries.

Keep Your Loved One's Name Alive

Four months after my son died I had my last name legally changed to his first name... Daniel. You may not want to go so far as to legally change your name, but you can find dozens of imaginative ways to keep your loved one's name alive. Use her nickname as one of your computer passwords, or start a business, charitable group or website using a variation of it. Engrave his name on a paving stone for your memorial garden, or hire a graphic artist to design a logo or icon for the name.

NOTES

[62] http://www.dyingconsciouslyboulder.com/aya-despacho/
[63] www.AfterlifeConference.com

Conclusion

I realize that the information contained in this book is not for everybody, especially the newly bereaved. I also acknowledge that this material is controversial. But controversy, like grief, can be perceived as a gift, because it makes us think, question and re-evaluate our reality.

Change, especially change brought on by trauma and loss, is certainly painful, but without pain as an ally, we would not stretch and grow. Pain causes us to shift our positions. It provides *traction*... something to push against, like a swimmer pushing off the edge of a pool. It creates propulsion, and propulsion to higher levels of awareness is what the soul craves, even though the ego fights fiercely against it. The soul says to pain, "Bring it on. Show me everything. Teach me. Take me. Expand me." The ego says, "Go away and leave me alone. I don't want to expand. I want to stay where everything is familiar." The soul reaches out for a vast vision of heaven. The ego finds a safe place to hunker down.

The ultimate healing message is this: *We do not die.* Love is the creative force of the universe, and it is indestructible.

In the words of my friend and shaman, Frank Coppieters:[64]

"Here, the storyline of the little self comes to a sudden stop, and you are welcomed by the forces of the unexpected.
It is brave to let go like this, surrendering, yielding, exploring, being comfortable in not knowing.

This is the territory of true love, pushing evolution forward.
The adventure of spirit is not limited to this earth.
It honors you as the cosmic occurrence you are.

The transformation has begun. It is taking you along.
Your heart is at the center of the transformation, and is so eager to cooperate. It had been designed always for this specific task."

---

[64] © 2014 - Frank Coppieters ,The Living Light Center

About the Author

Terri Daniel is an ordained interfaith minister, clinical chaplain and intuitive counselor who helps dying and grieving individuals discover a more spiritually spacious understanding of death and beyond. She is the author of *A Swan in Heaven: Conversations Between Two Worlds; Embracing Death: A New Look at Grief, Gratitude and God*; and *Turning the Corner on Grief Street: Loss and Bereavement as a Journey of Awakening.*

Terri teaches and conducts workshops at conferences and symposiums worldwide, offering a unique metaphysical perspective on birth, death and the afterlife via channeled teachings on religious history, spirituality and the journey of the soul. Her work includes facilitating bereavement support groups for children and adults, hospice and hospital chaplaincy, transition guidance, sacred ceremonies, death-awareness education and grief counseling.

In 2010 Terri founded the Afterlife Education Foundation and its annual conference, which features the world's leading researchers, counselors and educators in the metaphysics of death, dying and bereavement (www.afterlifeconference.com).

Terri resides in Portland, Oregon, with her dog Spootie.

CPSIA information can be obtained
at www.ICGtesting.com
Printed in the USA
BVHW070300030821
613056BV00001B/87